Additional Praises for Essentials of Cc

"The only thing better than Tracy Cc accountant and fraud investigator is her ability to reduce her real life experiences to writing. Tracy stands out as the only one who has ever been able to make the boring, dry subject of accounting fraud both entertaining and informative. She actually provides the reader who may possess little knowledge of the subject with a literal "how to uncover" fraud methodology. In short, Tracy Coenen is ZZZZ Best fraud investigator."

—Barry Minkow, Co-Founder of Fraud Discovery Institute

"*Essentials of Corporate Fraud* is unique among fraud books in that it provides decision-makers who aren't fraud experts with exactly the kind of "brass tacks" knowledge they need to meaningfully reduce their organizations' vulnerability to such crimes as embezzlement, fraudulent financial reporting, bribery, corruption and collusion. No fancy financial or accounting language. No convoluted theorizing about why fraud happens. Just well-founded actionable insight and advice on how to detect, prevent and investigate fraud—from someone who's been helping organizations protect themselves against white-collar crime for many years."

—Peter Goldmann, Editor and Publisher, *White-Collar Crime Fighter* newsletter.

"To be an effective auditor you have to first master forensic accounting. If there were more fraud professionals like Tracy Coenen around during my criminal career, I would have been forcibly retired many years earlier, or I may not have chosen the dark road to criminality all together."

—Sam E. Antar, Former Crazy Eddie CFO & convicted felon

"Tracy Coenen is one of the top fraud-fighters in America today, and her book is a must-read for everyone interested in corporate fraud. Her book is clear, concise and comprehensive in describing all of the major kinds of fraud, from embezzlement to boardroom chicanery. Filled with vivid examples that bring life to this difficult subject."

—Gary Weiss, author of *Born to Steal* and *Wall Street Versus America*

"Tracy Coenen's book is a must-read for anyone hoping to understand the psychology and methodology of white collar crime."

—*Zac Bissonnette, AOL Money & Finance's BloggingStocks.com*

"This book provides business professionals with an excellent overview of what is fraud, who commits fraud, indicators of fraudulent activity, common fraud schemes, and methods to prevent and detect fraud. Real-world examples illustrate and enhance the discussion of these various aspects of fraud. The book concludes with a very useful discussion of best practices in fraud management and the future of fraud. I would encourage any business executive interested in gaining a better understanding of fraud to read *Essentials of Corporate Fraud*."

—Michael D. Akers, Ph.D, CFE, CPA, Professor and Chair, Department of Accounting-Marquette University, Charles T. Horngren Professor of Accounting

"Coenen, widely recognized as 'the new breed' of forensic accountant, has authored the quintessential, text for business, legal and financial professionals on corporate fraud; an in depth examination of the subtle nuances, 'red flags,' and real issues associated with one of the hottest, and most financially devastating, business topics of the decade."

—Daniel W. Draz, M.S.,CFE, Adjunct Professor, Economic Crime Management Masters Program, Utica College/Adjunct Instructor, White Collar Crime & Fundamentals of Fraud, Portland State University

ESSENTIALS
of Corporate Fraud

Essentials Series

The Essentials Series was created for busy business advisory and corporate professionals. The books in this series were designed so that these busy professionals can quickly acquire knowledge and skills in core business areas.

Each book provides need-to-have fundamentals for those professionals who must:

- Get up to speed quickly, because they have been promoted to a new position or have broadened their responsibility scope.
- Manage a new functional area.
- Brush up on new developments in their area of responsibility.
- Add more value to their company or clients.

Other books in this series include

Essentials of Accounts Payable, Mary S. Schaeffer

Essentials of Balanced Scorecard, Mohan Nair

Essentials of Capacity Management, Reginald Tomas Yu-Lee

Essentials of Capital Budgeting, James Sagner

Essentials of Cash Flow, H.A. Schaeffer, Jr.

Essentials of Corporate Governance, Sanjay Anand

Essentials of Corporate Performance Measurement, George T. Friedlob, Lydia L.F. Schleifer, and Franklin J. Plewa, Jr.

Essentials of Cost Management, Joe and Catherine Stenzel

Essentials of Credit, Collections, and Accounts Receivable, Mary S. Schaeffer

Essentials of CRM: A Guide to Customer Relationship Management, Bryan Bergeron

Essentials of Financial Analysis, George T. Friedlob, and Lydia L.F. Schleifer

Essentials of Financial Risk Management, Karen A. Horcher

Essentials of Intellectual Property, Paul J. Lerner and Alexander I. Poltorak

Essentials of Knowledge Management, Bryan Bergeron

Essentials of Patents, Andy Gibbs and Bob DeMatteis

Essentials of Payroll Management and Accounting, Steven M. Bragg

Essentials of Sarbanes-Oxley, Sanjay Anand

Essentials of Shared Services, Bryan Bergeron

Essentials of Supply Chain Management, Michael Hugos

Essentials of Trademarks and Unfair Competition, Dana Shilling

Essentials of Treasury, Karen A. Horcher

Essentials of Managing Corporate Cash, Michele Allman-Ward and James Sagner

Essentials of XBRL, Bryan Bergeron

For more information on any of the foregoing titles, please visit our website at www.wiley.com.

ESSENTIALS
of Corporate Fraud

Tracy Coenen

WILEY

John Wiley & Sons, Inc.

Library of Congress Cataloging-in-Publication Data:

Coenen, Tracy, 1972-
    Essentials of corporate fraud / Tracy Coenen.
        p. cm.—(Essentials series)
    Includes index.
    ISBN 978-0-470-19412-6 (pbk.)
1. Corporations—Corrupt practices.   2. Fraud.   3. Fraud—Prevention.   I. Title.
    HV6768.C64 2008
    364.16'3—dc22   2007045811

Printed in the United States of America

10 9 8 7 6 5 4 3 2 1

For Max

Contents

Preface

Corporate fraud continues to fascinate the masses, yet companies as a whole have not been terribly effective in significantly decreasing the occurrence and cost of occupational fraud. While regulations have forced management to review policies and procedures, a wide-scale shift toward proactive fraud prevention has not occurred.

Understanding the root causes of fraud and learning about the most effective fraud prevention techniques are critical to reducing the incidence of corporate fraud. A long-term reduction in employee fraud is not achieved easily, yet a company that is committed to improving fraud prevention efforts can begin with some basic improvements.

This book is intended for executives, attorneys, and auditors who need a basic understanding of corporate fraud. It addresses some of the causes of fraud and the characteristics of those who commit fraud. The book examines warning signs of fraud within companies and the process of conducting a corporate fraud investigation. It further discusses opportunities for proactive fraud prevention, which include educating employees and implementing polices and procedures specifically designed to prevent fraud.

The topic of fraud is addressed broadly, as the book is intended to give an overview of fraud methods and results. Companies are best served by involving experienced anti-fraud professionals when they attempt to detect, investigate, and prevent fraud.

Acknowledgments

I offer my thanks to my family, friends, associates, and clients who have extended their support throughout my career. It has been quite a ride, and they have supported all of my efforts at marketing, public relations, professional development, and growing my fraud investigation practice. Without them, I would not be where I am today, professionally or personally.

A special thanks to those who love me unconditionally and cheer me on through all of life's challenges. You have made me stronger and have encouraged me to strive for more.

Thank you to Wiley for offering me this opportunity and for making the process so easy and enjoyable.

CHAPTER 1

The Fraud Problem

After reading this chapter, you will be able to

- Understand the results of fraud prevention efforts over the last several years.
- Identify the three main components of any fraud scheme, traditionally known as the fraud triangle.
- Discuss the various actions companies take against those who perpetrate fraud and the reasons why they do not initiate criminal prosecutions.

Internal fraud at companies is a big enough problem to be considered an industry unto itself. It is estimated that organizations lose an average of 5% of revenue annually to internal fraud, which equates to $652 billion in losses each year just in the United States.[1]

1

People often wonder why so much fraud occurs and why it is not caught sooner, thereby limiting the losses. The answer is simple. Companies have systems in place to help ensure that accounting transactions are recorded accurately and that proper procedures are followed. Companies have policies to guide the behavior of people who would generally strive to act in an ethical manner, but occasionally need rules to dictate their behavior. Those systems, procedures, and policies often work to catch errors and honest mistakes in the accounting process.

However, when an employee is committing fraud, he or she is deliberately trying to thwart those systems and policies. The person is purposely circumventing the system, while at the same time attempting to conceal his or her actions. While systems, policies, and procedures may be reasonably good at bringing errors to light, they typically cannot and do not expose fraud. Fraud constitutes a purposeful disregard for the system and a deliberate attempt to violate that system for personal gain, and most companies' systems aren't designed to stop this.

There are also the companies that have inadequate or nonexistent systems to ensure accurate accounting records and financial statements. Those companies can barely keep adequate and reliable records, even with honest employees. But if they can't even ensure a basic level of accuracy, management will hardly be able to prevent, detect, and stop fraud from within.

Internal fraud itself is troubling. Companies entrust their employees with assets, information, and customers. Business cannot be done unless companies put trust in people to sell their products or services, deliver them, collect the money, and keep accurate records.

Employees must be charged with growing and managing the business, as well as doing what is in the best interest of the owners and the rest of the company. When those trusted people steal, it can be disheartening. Maybe even more troubling is the fact that so little of the proceeds of fraud are ever recovered.

A 2006 fraud survey by KPMG[2] found that in 42% of major frauds, none of the stolen goods or money was recovered. None. The Association of Certified Fraud Examiners (ACFE) found equally disappointing results in its 2006 survey of fraud examiners. In 42% of internal fraud cases, there was no recovery of money or assets, and in 23% of cases, the recovery amounted to 25% or less of what was stolen.[3] As both of these studies show, close to half of internal fraud victims cannot count on recovering any of the proceeds of fraud, and another one-fourth will recover only a fraction of what was stolen. Clearly, companies cannot and should not expect to recover fraud proceeds.

Progress?

With the focus on fraud since the big cases of Enron, WorldCom, and Tyco, an important question is whether or not companies are making any progress in the fight against fraud. Has the focus on the fraud issue caused them to tighten controls and take swift action against perpetrators, or have companies remained largely complacent in fighting fraud?

The general consensus seems to be that companies have made some progress in protecting themselves against fraud, but still there has not been a noticeable decrease in fraud overall. Some might argue that the progress has not been swift enough, and that is why no real results have been seen. It also may be that companies have been so focused on compliance with Sarbanes–Oxley, that most of the measures taken are merely for the sake of compliance and not designed for true fraud prevention. Companies may think that they have improved in terms of fraud prevention and detection, but that self-assessment can often be overly optimistic. Until a marked decrease in fraud is seen worldwide, the idea that companies have been effective at reducing fraud is dubious.

The ACFE conducted studies on fraud detection, investigation, and prevention in 1996, 2002, 2004, and 2006. In each of these studies, Certified Fraud Examiners were asked to estimate the amount of revenue companies lose each year to internal fraud. In the 1996, 2002, and 2004 reports, Certified Fraud Examiners estimated that 6% of revenues would be lost by companies as a result of occupational fraud and abuse. When applied to the U.S. gross domestic product, that would total $600 billion in 2002[4] and $660 billion in 2003.[5]

Five percent of revenues were estimated to be lost to internal fraud in 2006,[6] a 1% decrease from previous estimates. When applied to the 2005 U.S. gross domestic product, this is an estimated $652 billion lost to occupational fraud. It's important to remember that these particular figures are all estimates and there is much room for error. The most important conclusion we can draw from these surveys is that professional fraud investigators don't think the instance of employee fraud has decreased to any great extent during the past several years.

And let us not forget that any estimate of the total cost of fraud is just that—an estimate. There is no way for anyone to know the exact total impact of fraud, because we know that a lot of fraud goes undetected. All we are left to do is make educated guesses about the total cost of fraud by assessing the frauds that were discovered and making assumptions about the frauds that were not discovered.

How Companies See Themselves

The results of the 2006 KPMG fraud study suggest that fraud risk management is becoming more important to companies, and it is of increased importance when companies engage in strategic planning. Companies recognize the importance of image and reputation, and this may be fueling a focus on reducing fraud scandals.[7]

The study further indicates that companies are devoting more time and resources to fraud management, with the focus generally on fraud detection and reporting. Less emphasis is being placed on fraud prevention and responses to the discovery of fraud. Survey participants reported an overall decrease in the average time it took to detect a fraud as a result of this greater focus on fraud detection.[8]

While the increased focus on fraud detection is a good thing, the lack of attention to fraud prevention and management's response to fraud is troubling. As we will see later, a swift response to fraud is necessary to deter other employees from committing fraud. And clearly, fraud prevention efforts can pay dividends if only management would value such activities.

A 2006 global survey by Ernst & Young had findings similar to those of the KPMG study. The firm's survey of more than 500 corporate leaders found that companies had increased their spending on assessing and improving internal controls. As a result, the corporate leaders believed they had made significant progress in detecting and preventing internal fraud.[9]

Although survey participants felt better positioned to detect and prevent fraud, there was little hard evidence to prove that fraud has been reduced. One out of five companies surveyed by Ernst & Young reported "significant fraudulent activity" within the past two years.

These surveys seem to have one common theme: Corporate executives think their companies are doing better now than in the recent past when it comes to preventing fraud, but none of the hard data supports that assertion. That's dangerous. Executives and management may very well be caught off guard by a fraud while they hold onto this false sense of security. Unless management can come to grips with the true effectiveness (or lack of effectiveness) of a company's fraud detection and prevention efforts, marked improvement cannot be made.

TIPS AND TECHNIQUES

How Companies See Themselves

Overall, companies see themselves as having made significant improvements in fraud prevention and detection during the past several years. However, fraud does not appear to have been reduced, according to studies by anti-fraud professionals. There is clearly a disconnect between actual performance and the executives' perception of their performance.

Defining Fraud

Occupational fraud and abuse goes by many other names, including internal fraud, employee fraud, employee theft, and embezzlement. The phrases "occupational fraud" or "internal fraud" are often preferable when discussing corporate fraud, because they apply to a range of employee misconduct while the other terms are a bit more restrictive.

In lay person's terms, occupational fraud is something that

- Violates a person's fiduciary duties to the organization.
- Is done in secret and concealed.
- Is done for a direct or indirect benefit to the perpetrator.
- Costs the employer assets, revenue, or opportunities.

Legally speaking, fraud is generally defined as an intentionally false representation about a material point, which causes a victim to suffer harm. Essentially, when someone purposely lies about an important fact and someone else loses money because of that lie, a fraud has been committed. Most of the instances of fraud are fairly straightforward to prove. After all, it's usually pretty clear when something is false, and whether it was material and there was a loss to a victim.

 TIPS AND TECHNIQUES

Legal Elements of Fraud

- Intentional
- False
- Representation
- Material point
- Victim suffers harm

It is not always so easy to prove intent. One of the first defenses that often surfaces in a fraud case is that the perpetrator simply made a mistake or error and there was no intent to defraud. In some situations, that may truly be the case. Plenty of errors are made daily in business, so that defense can't immediately be ruled out.

Fraud investigators, therefore, look for evidence of intent to defraud in the documents and actions of the accused. Manipulation of documents and evidence is often indicative of such intent. Innocent parties don't normally alter documents and conceal or destroy evidence. Although there may be times when these actions are taken to cover up a mistake due to fear of discipline, these things are usually perpetrated by those who had an active part in the fraud and its cover-up.

Obstruction of an investigation can also signal criminal intent on the part of a participant in a fraud scheme. Innocent parties don't usually lie or conceal information when being questioned relative to an occupational fraud. Naturally, employees are sometimes nervous or hesitant about providing information and evidence when fraud is being investigated. They may be reluctant to participate in an interview because of the fear of implicating others in the fraud. But again, innocent parties are, for the most part, not inclined to cover up evidence or lie about the situation. Therefore, false statements and other obstruction of an investigation can be another factor that points to the intent to defraud.

Finally, two additional factors to consider when determining the intent of an involved party are past behavior and the benefits obtained from the fraud. Employees, managers, and executives who have a prior history of engaging in unacceptable behavior or being involved in inappropriate transactions should be eyed carefully. Although past behavior doesn't prove fraud in a current investigation, a pattern of unethical behavior certainly indicates something about the character and tendencies of the accused.

It is important to determine whether an individual obtained any benefits from a suspected fraud. Typically, errors are exactly that—errors that don't personally benefit the person responsible. However, a transaction that creates a direct or indirect benefit for the person involved should be viewed as suspicious. Fraud is meant to give illegitimate benefits to the parties involved, and those benefits may be indicators of a participant's intent to defraud.

None of these factors alone can prove intent to defraud beyond all doubt. In the absence of a confession from the accused, intent may need to be established by compiling a list of behaviors that signal the intent. The more factors identified in the commission of a fraud, the closer we come to proving that a fraudster intended to commit the crime.

Fraud Triangle

One of the most basic concepts in the field of fraud examination originated with the famous criminologist, Donald R. Cressey. While doing research for his doctoral thesis in the 1950s, Cressey developed the following hypothesis about fraud:

> Trusted persons become trust violators when they conceive of themselves as having a financial problem which is nonsharable, are aware this problem can be secretly resolved by violation of the position of financial trust, and are able to apply to their own conduct in that situation verbalizations which enable them to adjust their conceptions of themselves as trusted

persons with their conceptions of themselves as users of the entrusted funds or property.[10]

Quite simply put, Cressey's hypothesis states that three key elements are present in every internal fraud: motivation, opportunity, and rationalization. These three elements have become known as the "fraud triangle." Contemporary academics and investigators have added their own ideas to modify this concept, but the fraud triangle is still the most widely recognized basic framework of fraud.

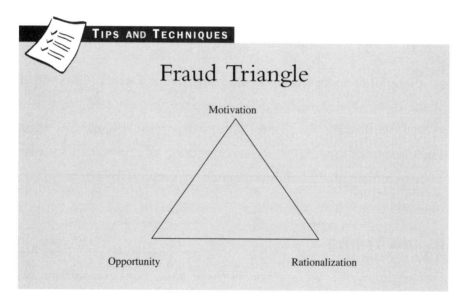

TIPS AND TECHNIQUES

Fraud Triangle

Motivation

Opportunity

Rationalization

Motivation

The motivation component of fraud or embezzlement is the pressure or "need" that a person feels. It could be a true financial need, such as the need to replace belongings after a house fire. Other real needs may include financial distress from a lost job, high medical bills, child support payments, investment losses, or heavy personal debt.

The motivation could also be a *perceived* financial need, whereby a person strongly desires material goods but doesn't have the money or means to acquire them. A person may also have an addiction such as gambling or drugs, and that could be a motivator. Nonfinancial pressures and motivators may be in play as well, and these could include such things as the expectation for good results at work, the imposition of unachievable goals, or the need to cover up a poorly performed job. Any pressure in one's business or personal life could conceivably motivate someone to commit occupational fraud.

IN THE REAL WORLD

Gambling as a Motivation for Fraud

Looking back over the past 10 or 20 years, it may have been unusual to hear about a fraud scheme in which the perpetrator had a gambling addiction. Today, anecdotal evidence suggests that this is occurring more and more often.

Opportunities for gambling are increasing as casinos open across the country. Gambling is now recognized as an addiction that is not too different from alcohol or drugs. It can be a strong motivator to commit fraud, as casinos are clearly set up in order to make the gamblers lose. It's a habit that gets expensive very quickly.

Further complicating the problem is the belief on the part of many problem gamblers that one day they will win big and will pay back the theft from the company. This makes it much easier for an employee to justify the theft in her or his mind.

Opportunity

The opportunity to commit fraud includes the access to assets, people, information, and computer systems that enables the person not only to commit the fraud but to conceal it. Employees are given all sorts of access to assets and records in order to carry out their job duties, and that access is one of the key components of fraud. This is why it is so important to limit employees' access to only the assets, systems, and information that are necessary for them to properly perform their jobs.

As corporate structures have become more complex and managers have become responsible for a wider range of employees and functions, individual employees have been given more access and control. Increased access to resources and data, along with increased control over functional areas of companies, has created a situation in which it may be easier than ever to commit occupational fraud. Obviously, these increased opportunities to commit fraud involve risk, but in many ways they are unavoidable in the modern business world.

Rationalization

The third and final piece of the fraud triangle is rationalization. This is the process by which an employee determines that the fraudulent behavior is "okay" in her or his mind. For those with deficient moral codes, the process of rationalization is easy. For those with higher moral standards, it may not be quite so easy; they may have to convince themselves that a fraud is okay by creating "excuses" in their minds. A thief may convince himself that his theft just makes up for the bonus or raise that he should have received but did not. An embezzler may tell herself that she is just "borrowing" money from the company and that she will eventually pay it back. Maybe the rationalization is that no one will "miss" the funds or assets, or that the company "deserves" the theft because of lax supervision and security.

Management has the most control over the opportunity portion of the fraud triangle. It can limit access to assets and put controls in place that ensure monitoring of systems and people. Motivation can be constrained by management as well, although not to the degree that opportunity can be limited. The best way to reduce "needs" is by paying employees fairly (to reduce perceived financial burdens) and by creating performance systems that are reasonable (not requiring job performance beyond what is realistic).

Rationalization is probably the most dangerous piece of the fraud triangle because it is the one that companies have the least control over. It is nearly impossible for management to eliminate the rationalization piece because they can't control the minds of employees. Management has no way of knowing what lies an employee may tell himself in order to justify fraud in his mind, so there is virtually no way of counteracting the lies.

Characteristics of Internal Fraud

Employee fraud falls into at least one of three widely recognized general categories:

1. Asset misappropriation

2. Bribery and corruption

3. Financial statement fraud

Many fraud schemes include components from more than one of these three categories.

On average, an internal fraud scheme lasts 18 months and costs a company $159,000.[11] Almost one-fourth of the cases studied in the ACFE's 2006 *Report to the Nation* caused losses over $1 million.[12]

When two or more employees collude to commit an internal fraud, the losses to the company are more than four times higher than the losses from a single-person fraud.[13] The losses are dramatically higher when employees collude, because they are able to jointly cover up the fraud. A company with good supervision of employees and cross-checking of work may still fall victim to a fraud scheme if the right employees collude to cover one another's tracks. This collusion also increases the length of time a fraud scheme may continue without being detected.

Smaller companies are generally hit harder by fraud than larger companies. Their median dollar loss per fraud scheme is higher than in larger companies, and naturally, smaller companies have smaller budgets, which consequently feel an even greater impact from fraud.[14]

Detecting Internal Fraud

According to the 2006 study by the ACFE, 34% of frauds are detected through a tip from an employee, vendor, customer, or anonymous person.[15] This supports the idea of having anonymous hotlines available for people to report fraud, which will be discussed further on. If people are willing to report suspected fraud to the company, it makes sense to make it as easy as possible to report the suspicious behavior.

TIPS AND TECHNIQUES

How Fraud Is Discovered[a]

Tip: 34.2%

By Accident: 25.4%

Internal Audit: 20.2%

Internal Controls: 19.2%

External Audit: 12.0%

Notified by Police: 3.8%

Note: Some frauds had more than one reported method of discovery, causing the percentages here to exceed 100%.

―――――

[a]2006 Report to the Nation, Association of Certified Fraud Examiners, Austin, TX.

The next most common way to detect internal fraud is by accident. About 25% of frauds are detected this way.[16] An accidental detection may include a phone call routed to the wrong person, who then uncovers the fraud, or a piece of mail that is inadvertently intercepted, or some other chance event that causes an outside party to become aware of fraudulent activities. This statistic about accidental detection is very disturbing to fraud prevention professionals. In spite of all of the anti-fraud resources available to companies and the increased fraud prevention efforts management says are being undertaken, one-fourth of frauds are still discovered by accident.

Following closely behind in the fraud detection spectrum are internal audits and internal controls. Some may be surprised that these methods of detecting fraud end up in third and fourth place, given that they are often considered highly effective methods of preventing fraud. It is quite possible that companies still haven't developed internal controls sufficiently to make them as effective as they might be.

TIPS AND TECHNIQUES

Fraud Tips by Source[a]

Tips about internal fraud don't come only from employees. Outside parties can be a valuable source of credible fraud tips.

Employee: 64.1% of tips

Anonymous: 18.1% of tips

Customer: 10.7% of tips

Vendor: 7.1% of tips

[a]2006 Report to the Nation, Association of Certified Fraud Examiners, Austin, TX.

Why Audits Don't Find More Fraud

Users of financial statements often mistakenly believe that independent auditors are charged with finding fraud. If the auditors signed off on the financial statements, there must not be fraud. That couldn't be further from the truth, and boards of directors, investors, banks, and executives need to understand the real purpose of audits.

Audits by independent auditors are not designed to detect fraud, and most often they do not detect fraud that may be present. Instead, an audit is aimed only at determining whether the financial statements are free from material misstatements. That is, are the financial statements fairly presented, and do they give an accurate picture of the known financial condition of the company? The auditors test only a small number of transactions in this quest to audit the financial statements, and they will direct management to correct any material errors that are found during that testing.

In no way are auditors required to look for fraud in a company. They are required to be aware of the potential for fraud, to discuss ways fraud could be committed, and to exercise professional skepticism when auditing the books and records. If they come across evidence that may suggest that fraud is occurring, the auditors have some responsibility to look into those matters and report their findings to management or the board of directors. This is a fairly low level of responsibility, so outside auditors cannot be relied on to find fraud in companies.

Taking Action

Companies that fall victim to occupational fraud have several choices to make after the fraud has been discovered. First, the company must decide how much to investigate and who should do the investigating. But once the investigation results are in, the important choices need to be made.

Something has to be done about the employee or employees involved in the fraud. If no action is taken, it sets a bad precedent for other employees. Studies have found that when employees perceive that fraud is being detected and corrective action is taken, there can be a general deterrent effect. For this reason, employees need to know that there are fair and swift consequences for those who commit fraud.

If the company decides to punish the fraud perpetrator, the question remains how far to take the punishment. On one end of the spectrum is discipline, with the perpetrator remaining employed by the company. The discipline may be formal or informal and may include some agreement to repay the fraud proceeds.

Somewhere in the middle of the spectrum, the employee is terminated from the company. On the far end of the spectrum is legal action, either civil or criminal or both. Of course, litigation is expensive, and we've already seen that the likelihood of recovering the proceeds of fraud is low.

Criminal prosecution is many times difficult to initiate, inasmuch as local, state, and federal law enforcement agencies are always busy and seem to want to pursue only the largest or most egregious cases. Companies can often increase the likelihood of a criminal prosecution if they are willing to do a lot of the hard work at their own expense. A fully investigated case with well-organized evidence is much more appealing to law enforcement agencies than a case with many allegations but little substantive evidence uncovered.

Failing to Take Action

Plenty of companies take little or no legal action against perpetrators of occupational fraud. The ACFE asked why companies didn't refer their fraud cases to law enforcement. The most common reason was the fear of bad publicity, which accounted for 43% of cases. Thirty-three percent of cases were not pursued because management believed that internal discipline was sufficient. Thirty percent of cases were not pursued because a private settlement was reached, and 21% of cases were deemed too costly to pursue. Note also that some cases had more than one reason reported, causing the sum of the percentages to exceed 100%.[17]

Often companies just want to move forward and put the fraud in the past, particularly if it involved highly visible employees. Taking action against those who commit occupational fraud prolongs the pain and is an ongoing reminder of the fraud. That prospect is not appealing to many corporate managers and likely accounts for many of the companies that don't pursue employees who have stolen from them.

Why It Is Easy to Commit Fraud

Fraud can often be fairly easy to commit. Why is that so? One of the major reasons is that employers must put trust in their employees and give them access to data and assets. It's also important to remember that employers give responsibility to people who are trusted. If someone wasn't deemed trustworthy enough to take money to the bank, she or he wouldn't be handed the bank deposit. That trust inherently means that opportunities to commit fraud are handed to employees each day.

IN THE REAL WORLD

Trusting Employees

A family-owned manufacturing firm with a 15-year history of success was interested in growing significantly. One important strategic step was the hiring of a chief financial officer (CFO). Up until that point, the finance function was managed with a combination of an in-house bookkeeper, an outside accounting firm, and the financial knowledge of the owner, who was an engineer.

Immediately after being hired, the new CFO began making changes to the finance procedures. The owners went along with all of it, believing that he had the best interest of the company at heart. Besides, he came highly recommended and was hired for his expertise in finance. He knew what he was doing!

The truth is that all of the CFO's changes were done to take information and control away from the owners while he was stealing everything the company owned. Any objection to new procedures or lack of information was met with an "I'm the finance professional" response.

In less than three years, the CFO succeeded at bankrupting the company while lining his own pockets with enough money to retire and live comfortably for the rest of his life.

The way modern business is conducted can contribute to the fraud problem. Managers are supervising many people and can't possibly watch over all of them. Some employees work offsite or telecommute, making supervision of them more difficult. Lack of real loyalty in the business world may contribute to the fraud problem because employees may have an easier time rationalizing bad acts.

Employees naturally become well educated on the inner workings of a company. They analyze portions of the company's business process day after day. They know where the gaps and weaknesses are.

They often know what will be reviewed by management and what will not. They are so close to their work that they are able to devise methods for concealing fraud. They see the details of their work each day and become intimately familiar with their part of the business. It is not difficult to find a way to exploit the system.

The fact that fraud is easy to commit is no excuse for employees to scam their employers. But executives and managers must become aware of the potential for fraud and must acknowledge the risk of fraud and the ease with which it may be committed.

Fraud-Fighting Lessons

As you will learn throughout the rest of this book, there is much work to be done by companies that want to reduce opportunities for fraud. Although the concept of internal controls goes back many years, management still has a lot of room for improvement. Specifically, internal controls at many companies need to be adjusted so that they better address fraud risks. Whereas internal controls at one time may have been primarily directed at preventing errors in the accounting system, in today's world those controls should focus on preventing fraud.

Companies that have anti-fraud programs in place also have room for improvement. The anti-fraud programs need to be more wide reaching and comprehensive. Comprehensive fraud prevention programs involve all levels of employees and should integrate internal controls with anti-fraud education and a formal ethics policy. It is clear that the current fraud prevention efforts of companies have not been effective, and this book aims to assist executives, attorneys, and auditors in learning the critical facts about fraud detection, investigation, and prevention.

Notes

1. 2006 Report to the Nation, Association of Certified Fraud Examiners, Austin, TX.
2. 2006 Fraud Survey by KPMG, an Australian partnership and a member firm of the KPMG network of independent member firms affiliated with KPMG International, a Swiss cooperative.
3. 2006 Report to the Nation, Association of Certified Fraud Examiners, Austin, TX.
4. 2002 Report to the Nation, Association of Certified Fraud Examiners, Austin, TX.
5. 2004 Report to the Nation, Association of Certified Fraud Examiners, Austin, TX.
6. 2006 Report to the Nation, Association of Certified Fraud Examiners, Austin, TX.
7. 2006 Fraud Survey by KPMG.
8. Ibid.
9. 9th Global Fraud Survey: Fraud Risk in Emerging Markets, Ernst & Young, completed in 2006.
10. Cressey, Donald R., Other People's Money: A Study in the Social Psychology of Embezzlement, 1953 Edition. Boston: Wadsworth Publishing Co., 1972.
11. 2006 Report to the Nation, Association of Certified Fraud Examiners, Austin, TX.

12. Ibid.

13. Ibid.

14. Ibid.

15. Ibid.

16. Ibid.

17. Ibid.

CHAPTER 2

People Who Commit Fraud

After reading this chapter, you will be able to

- Understand the relationship between an employee's position within a company and the frauds the person can commit.

- Identify personal red flags of fraud that may indicate a potential fraud problem with an employee.

- Differentiate between senior management fraud and front-line employee fraud.

Aren't people who commit fraud all the same? They're dishonest types who are greedy by nature. They are deceitful in general, so by hiring honest people, companies are protected from theft. Right? Wrong.

Those who commit occupational fraud tend to have many similar characteristics, but they're not all quite as easy to spot or as common as many people would think. Understanding what motivates employees to steal from companies is the key to detecting and preventing internal fraud. Understanding the opportunities available for fraud at the various employment levels is helpful as well. Knowledge is power, and although just knowing about thieves and their characteristics won't prevent them from stealing, it is certainly a step toward improving fraud prevention efforts and internal controls.

Is identifying common characteristics in fraudsters akin to stereotyping people? I hope not. Management should be able to use these common characteristics to identify potential problem people and problem situations. There are no absolutes regarding the characteristics of those who commit fraud. Rather, there are some common characteristics that have been identified by fraud investigators and anti-fraud professionals. The identification of these characteristics should be a tool in the fight against fraud, but not necessarily a hard-and-fast rule.

The Facts

The Association of Certified Fraud Examiners (ACFE) has been conducting regular surveys of fraud investigators during the past decade to determine who commits fraud, how it is done, what common schemes occur, and how companies detect and pursue fraud matters. Survey respondents are Certified Fraud Examiners who have investigated cases of internal fraud and are willing to provide many details about the cases. From these detailed responses, the ACFE has compiled some very revealing statistics.

Maybe the single most important statistic cited in the 2006 survey about those who commit internal fraud is this: 92% have no prior criminal charges or convictions related to fraud.[1] Even though we can do a criminal records check to weed out undesirable employees before they are hired, it's important to understand that those who commit theft and embezzlement while on the job often don't even have a criminal record. We may rely on clues to tip us off that fraud may be occurring, yet one of the most basic clues—a prior record—is most often not present in internal fraud.

Violent criminals often make it easy for us to spot them, developing criminal histories of an increasingly serious nature. White collar criminals usually don't do us any such favors by dropping hints about themselves. They often have completely clean records that don't indicate any tendency to commit crimes.

Does this mean companies should stop doing criminal background checks? Absolutely not. They're still an important part of weeding out bad actors. A company will still hire people who may later steal, yet it is undeniably important at least to do the criminal records check to identify those with prior histories. It's one more weapon in the anti-fraud arsenal.

Position Equals Power

The amount of money lost to an internal corporate fraud is most significantly influenced by the perpetrator's position in the organization.

When we look at various characteristics of those committing fraud, this makes sense, because access creates opportunity. Typically, the higher a person moves in a company, the greater access she or he is granted to information, assets, data, and people. That creates more opportunities to commit fraud.

Men and women commit a fairly equal number of frauds at work. The most recent ACFE survey indicated that 61% of fraud schemes were perpetrated by men, while 39% were committed by women.[2] The 2004 ACFE survey put the differential at 53% committed by men and 47% by women,[3] while the 2002 survey cited that internal fraud was committed 54% by men and 47% by women.[4] These differences are not terribly significant. Overall, the consensus is that men and women participate in a fairly equal number of fraud schemes.

Of note, however, is the magnitude of those schemes. Men participate in much more costly frauds. The most recent ACFE survey puts the median fraud loss from a male-perpetrated scheme at $250,000, whereas the median loss from a female-perpetrated scheme is only $120,000.[5] This indicates that the frauds committed by men are more than twice as expensive. The 2002 and 2004 ACFE surveys put the losses from frauds committed by men at about three times higher than those committed by women.

This difference between the genders is probably related to the fact that men still hold a proportionately higher number of senior management positions. Those higher positions offer more access to opportunities to commit and conceal fraud.

As you may expect, tenure, age, and education are also closely related to larger frauds. The more expensive internal frauds are committed by the more tenured, the older, and the more educated.

As with gender, these more costly frauds are likely due to the greater access to people, information, assets, and computer systems that will facilitate a fraud and its subsequent cover-up.

The higher the position in the company, the more access to data, records, and personnel the employee has. This, in turn, can lead to a larger fraud. Consider a senior-level executive who has access to almost all information in a company. This might make fraud easier to commit. The same executive also wields power over many employees, so the opportunity to cover up a fraud or intimidate someone who asks questions is more likely.

The data confirms that the largest fraud losses are caused by executives. They commit frauds that are 4.5 times more expensive than those committed by managers.[6] The disparity between executive frauds and those committed by front-line employees is even greater, with executive frauds almost 13 times more expensive.[7]

It is often easiest to focus on the visible frauds committed by low-level employees. Everyone can comprehend the idea of a dishonest teenager stealing from a cash register. It's not so easy to believe that a long-term, trusted management employee is committing fraud. Yet these less visible frauds need to receive more attention, because clearly they cost companies the most.

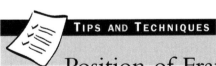

TIPS AND TECHNIQUES

Position of Fraud Perpetrator[a]

The median loss from a fraud perpetrated by[8]

Employee: $78,000

Tips and Techniques (continued)

Manager: $218,000

Owner or Executive: $1,000,000

[a]2006 Report to the Nation, Association of Certified Fraud Examiners, Austin, TX.

Personal Red Flags of Fraud

There are hundreds of personal characteristics or situations that may indicate a greater likelihood of committing fraud, or that may be signals of a fraud in progress. It is important to be aware of these traits and circumstances in order to head off fraud early. The existence of one, or two, or a few of these conditions certainly isn't proof positive of a fraud in progress. However, as more of these red flags are identified, the likelihood of a fraud increases and an investigation may be warranted.

Lifestyle Issues

There are some common lifestyle themes in those who commit occupational fraud. Most commonly, a noticeable and significant change in lifestyle can be a red flag of fraud. The obvious question that is raised is: Where did this newfound wealth come from? Clearly, an employee who is suddenly wearing expensive watches and jewelry or driving an expensive car or motorcycle has something unusual happening. It is possible that there is an explanation for the expensive possessions, but inheritances or other large windfalls are rare. Thieves may use the "inheritance excuse" often, but reality demonstrates something else.

Many occupational thieves cannot help but flaunt their new-found wealth. While conventional wisdom may suggest that someone who is stealing from the company might be best off hiding the proceeds, logic and reason do not always play a part in fraud.

One executive recounts the story of the company's bookkeeper, who showed up for work on a brand new Harley-Davidson motorcycle. Management knew her salary wasn't enough to warrant the purchase of such an expensive toy, but they ignored the signal this should have sent. Many months later, it was discovered that the bookkeeper had defrauded the company of hundreds of thousands of dollars. Imagine the different outcome if they had paid attention to the warning sign and investigated immediately.

It is important to be aware of these lifestyle changes, not only when they occur suddenly, but also when they occur over a sustained period of time. While it's not possible to know everything about a family's finances, it is possible to get a sense of the earnings capacity of an employee and spouse. When the family lives beyond the known means and appears to outpace the earning capacity, it is cause for concern.

Outpacing earnings capacity does not necessarily mean that an employee is stealing from the company, although that is the first question that should be raised. If an employee is not stealing to purchase those possessions, it is possible that she or he is incurring debt to finance them. Excessive debt levels can become a motivator for fraud, so this is of concern as well.

This particular issue can become more difficult to "diagnose" when it relates to senior management. With large salaries, bonuses, and perks dished out regularly, it may be hard to estimate an appropriate level of legitimate possessions for a senior-level executive. Certainly an affluent lifestyle is the norm for those employees, so attempting to draw accurate conclusions about their job-related honesty on the basis of lifestyle and possessions would be difficult, if not impossible.

Longstanding financial difficulties can be a red flag for fraud as well. High debts, bad credit, child support or alimony issues, or general money mismanagement could all end up being motivators for fraud. They all create a "need" in the employee, which could ultimately be filled with money from the employer. Companies must never underestimate a "need" for money, whether that need is real or only perceived.

It seems that in this modern economy, people are more anxious to buy material goods than ever before. The desire to keep up with the neighbors or outdo the coworker sometimes outweighs the ability of the family to afford the goods. As unlikely as it may seem to people who would never steal, these desires can lead to fraud. All sorts of justifications can be created in one's mind when there is a strong enough desire to have the money that will fund the lifestyle.

IN THE REAL WORLD

A History of Financial Problems

A family-owned construction company with a longstanding, successful history hired its first non-family executive. He did well, and the company flourished, but he was fired after almost 10 years with the company; he was the mastermind behind an elaborate fraud scheme that cost the company more than $12 million.

Personal Problems

The most obvious personal problems that could be red flags of fraud are issues surrounding addiction. This includes addiction to drugs and alcohol as well as to gambling. KPMG's 2006 Fraud Survey, conducted in Australia and New Zealand, found that "greed and lifestyle considerations, together with gambling, were the most common motivators of fraud."[9] Aside from the obvious expense of the addiction itself, it often causes further financial distress through absences and poor performance at work.

How does one know if a coworker or a subordinate is caught up in an addiction? It might not be possible to know for sure. But if warning signs are there, it makes sense for management to simply keep an eye on the employee and the employee's work product. It doesn't mean that a potential addiction deserves a full-blown fraud investigation. It merely means that the supervision of the employee should be stepped up a little, either on an informal or a formal basis, depending on the severity of the warning signs.

A criminal background can be a red flag of fraud. Past criminal behavior could be an indicator of the propensity to commit fraud in the future. However, as we've already learned, many who commit fraud are first-time offenders. So the correlation between prior criminality and fraud is not necessarily definitive, but it would be foolish to totally ignore the existence of a criminal past.

Chronic legal problems in general can be a warning sign in employees. As with many of the other causes for concern, legal troubles can quickly become expensive. Any situation that puts an unusual amount of financial stress on an employee could be the catalyst for fraud.

Legal problems can also help highlight people who create or attract trouble. That may sound unfair, but it still bears mentioning. There are certain people in the world who seem to attract trouble wherever they go. Those troubles aren't necessarily turned "off" when the employee enters the workplace. This is one of those warning signs that may indicate a problem employee and call for additional supervision of that worker.

Unfortunately, infidelity can also be related to corporate fraud. On one hand, infidelity can be very expensive. A cheating husband needs to purchase dinners, flowers, and gifts with money that his wife will not miss. Where will those funds come from? On-the-job fraud can be one option, as it provides funds that a spouse wouldn't miss. And on the other hand, the deception involved in infidelity certainly indicates a willingness to be deceitful in general. The compromised morals of a cheating spouse cannot be ignored as such behavior relates to the potential to lie to and steal from an employer.

The most common general cause for concern when assessing the potential for fraud is instability. Instability in connection with a person's family or with employment and earnings can cause that person to turn to fraud. A good rule of thumb is to ask yourself: "Could this be expensive?" If so, you may have the first part of the fraud triangle previously discussed—the motivation to commit fraud.

Personal Risk Factors for Fraud

Known financial problems

Obvious change in lifestyle

Addictions—alcohol, drugs, gambling

Criminal background

Chronic legal problems

Infidelity

Instability in personal life

Attitudes on the Job

Assessing an employee's attitude on the job and drawing conclusions about the likelihood of fraud are very subjective. These are not hard-and-fast rules, nor are they meant to be stereotypes. Rather, they are just certain characteristics that owners and managers of defrauded companies have found to be typical of in fraudsters. In looking back at those who stole from the companies, many items on this list were identified as traits of the person stealing.

Certainly, taking one trait or attitude and trying to draw a conclusion from it would be misguided. For example, what accountant or lawyer doesn't work long days? It would be irresponsible to draw a conclusion about those professionals just by looking at the one habit of being the first employee in and the last employee to leave.

However, it is important to be attentive to multiple red flags of fraud in one person. Those at-risk traits and characteristics should at least be warning signs that cause management to take notice. It is good business to be on the lookout for potential problems with employees. So when management detects several red flags of fraud within a person, and then notices that the employee is working unusually long hours, that may merit further investigation.

One of the most common characteristics to look for in at-risk employees is an overall weak code of ethics. If a person is willing to engage in dishonest behavior in other parts of her or his life, who's to say she or he won't be dishonest at work? It's even more troubling when a person boasts about dishonest behavior and the benefits obtained by engaging in it. Listen carefully to conversations and look for clues that indicate the employee condones or participates in unethical behavior. Dishonest behavior is a huge warning sign.

Another common trait in occupational fraudsters is a constant attempt to work "outside" the system. This means not following the rules that everyone else abides by, not following established procedures, and generally trying to beat the system. Look for the person who believes the rules don't apply to her or him, or is always trying to find a way around the rules for her or his own personal benefit.

Work Habits

Work habits of individuals who commit fraud also show some telltale signs. At-risk employees may have a history of poor work performance coupled with rationalization or justification of that poor performance. Employees who might be more likely to commit fraud also sometimes have a track record of shirking responsibility for substandard performance. An employee with these attitudes may more easily justify a fraud in her or his mind.

Equally as troubling may be the employee who is desperately trying to improve performance or meet certain targets. While goals and benchmarks are necessary in the workplace, a laser focus on these by an employee who has a recent history of poor performance could indicate a disposition to fraud. Even an employee who has always had an excellent level of performance can succumb to fraud in order to maintain the appearance of that high level of performance. Particularly when an employee's job is at stake, it is easy to see that the motivation to inflate numbers may exist.

Dishonest employees have been known to become overly protective of data and documents under their control. They may be reluctant to share information with coworkers or even managers. They may keep tight control of certain documents and never let them out of their sight. They might be unwilling to swap tasks with another employee, even temporarily. Employees engaging in theft also may be unwilling to train anyone else to do their job duties. These employees may be unusually uncooperative with the auditors when asked for supporting documentation.

Chronic dissatisfaction with the employee's position, duties, coworkers, or supervisors is also cause for concern. Employees who feel unfairly treated or who feel persecuted on the job can more easily justify stealing from the company. They can often feel that the company or the department of the manager "deserves" to become a victim of fraud. Equally at risk for fraud is the employee who believes it is okay to steal to settle a score or supplement a perceived pay imbalance. A dissatisfied or disgruntled employee is more likely to rationalize a fraud as payback to the company.

Look for unusual behaviors on the job. Most broadly, a sudden and significant change in behavior can signal a problem. For example, an employee who is usually on time and relatively cheerful at work may suddenly start showing up late and seem unhappy. This isn't necessarily indicative of fraud, but it might point to personal problems that could indirectly influence an employee theft. A change in behavior might not be a sign of fraud immediately, but it may indicate other lifestyle issues that management should watch. As previously mentioned, those types of problems can be catalysts for fraud.

Other unusual behaviors include always being the first employee in or the last one out. The employee who looks for an excuse to linger at work in order to be alone could pose a problem. Similarly, an employee who never takes a vacation may cause concern. Companies have uncovered many frauds when employees who were regularly on the job had an unexpected illness or unexpected absence. It is during such an absence that fraud can be uncovered, because the employee is not there to cover all bases. Thus, someone who doesn't want to take planned time off may be covering up a fraud scheme.

Some employees engaged in fraud schemes will take vacations or medical leaves, but this time off is often carefully planned and leads to tremendous anxiety for the employee. An absence requires orchestration of the work duties. Most commonly, the employee who is stealing will attempt to insulate herself or himself from other employees in the department. No one is allowed to "take over" the job duties while she or he is on leave. If some duties absolutely must be handled by someone else during the absence, the specific duties are laid out very carefully. The dishonest employee may also frequently call in to check on the person overseeing those tasks.

TIPS AND TECHNIQUES

Inexpensive Ways to Detect Fraud

Two classic fraud prevention techniques are mandatory vacations and periodic job rotations. Mandatory vacations of one week or more (consecutively) are helpful, because the employee cannot continuously monitor a fraud scheme while away. Job rotations are also effective at disrupting these schemes, especially when the employees are not given advance notice.

Often overlooked when considering the potential for fraud is a manager who does subordinate-level work. While it may be reasonable that a supervisor or other manager may "fill in" for an absent employee or a vacant position, it is not reasonable that the supervisor or manager would do a subordinate's duties for the long term. Doing these subordinate-level duties for an extended period of time may indicate a manager who is engaging in a fraud scheme and maintaining control of the lower-level tasks in order to cover up the fraud.

IN THE REAL WORLD

Unusual Work Habits

The CFO of a healthcare organization had divisional controllers who were responsible for overseeing various locations in the United

In general, those looking for fraud should be aware that over time employees become familiar with the company's operations. Like it or not, they can easily formulate ways to cover up a fraud, especially if they are in a position of trust. It's critical to remember that employees are not necessarily above testing the system. Additionally, close associations with people inside the company can facilitate fraud and the process of covering up fraud. These red flags need to be carefully examined whenever they arise.

Senior Management

It is easy to focus on the fraud that we see, which is most commonly the smaller thefts committed by front-line employees. It's easy to talk about installing security cameras to stop inventory theft, because it is something tangible that everyone can see and relate to. It's not so easy to talk about putting in place safeguards to thwart potential fraud by the man or woman who signs the paychecks.

Fraud by upper-level executives is often not tangible to most people in and around a company. Many might not even understand what financial statement fraud is. (I was even asked by a CPA whether anyone is actually harmed by a financial statement fraud. Of course people and entities are harmed by financial statement fraud!)

But it's clear to those of us in the "fraud industry" that fraud by senior management is important because of the huge cost it entails, not to mention its other "side effects," which are discussed elsewhere in this book. So while it's easier to focus on the smaller frauds by front-line employees, it is more important to focus on the serious fraud committed by management because it happens daily, all around us.

Many wonder how the attitudes and characteristics of senior-level executive thieves differ from those of lower-level employees. At the core, they can be very much the same. Greed is greed. Small greed may look a little different from big greed, but it is still characterized by the same desire and the same motivation.

Where senior-management fraudsters distinguish themselves is the depth of their greed and arrogance. They often take these to a whole new level. Consider some high-profile executives who were tried, convicted, and sent to prison. Often these executives can't help but exhibit these traits quite openly.

Executive fraudsters typically have highly material personal values, and they are likely to flaunt their wealth and possessions. Success for this type of thief is almost always measured in financial terms. Professional accomplishments outside of monetary gains are not valued nearly as highly.

Senior Management Attitudes

Bernie Ebbers of WorldCom was a lavish spender who thought that a code of conduct was a waste of time. His behavior provided an unfortunate example for other executives at WorldCom. Additionally, the culture at the company dictated that senior-level executives were never challenged on questionable accounting applications or inappropriate items.

The company was always in "deal mode," and the numerous acquisitions made it hard for outsiders to compare current numbers against relevant historic numbers. Certainly the attitude of Mr. Ebbers relating to ethical behavior tainted other executives, and it ultimately led to a massive $11 billion accounting scandal.

The interpersonal relationships of executives who commit fraud are often strained or nonexistent. People are frequently treated as objects and not individuals, and these executives are usually extremely self-centered, with few friends. They are often hostile to employees or peers who challenge their ideas, and they are known for playing favorites among subordinates. Even though loyalty is demanded from subordinates, the executive is loyal to no one except herself or himself.

Professionally, peers and competitors often do not like the top management defrauder. The executive speaks often about her or his achievements, but rarely discusses losses or failure. Facts are often embellished to make achievements look even more impressive.

Senior Management Behavior

"Chainsaw Al" Dunlap of Sunbeam fame is an example of how easily a large-scale fraud can be perpetrated by an executive. He rescued many companies from the brink of disaster, so when he started at Sunbeam the same was expected.

Everyone knew of Dunlap's reputation for slashing payroll and closing plants, but these actions were welcomed by companies that needed a major turnaround. However, the cuts at Sunbeam went so deep that the company had difficulty functioning even at a core level. Many of the company's costs increased as a result of Dunlap's cuts, and the outlook was grim.

Yet the company's stock was soaring, in large part based on Dunlap's reputation for turnaround success. Dunlap created outrageous financial expectations and pushed employees to do the impossible, bringing Sunbeam to the brink of collapse.

Employees eventually produced the numbers Dunlap wanted or found themselves unemployed. Fraud was accepted, and employees who didn't play the game didn't stay long. Financial statement fraud was committed to meet the numbers Dunlap promised Wall Street. The entire scheme eventually unraveled.

Encouraging or Discouraging Fraud

Maybe the single most effective way to prevent fraud committed by employees is to create a corporate culture that places a high value on ethical behavior. Doesn't that sound like the same old "solution" we've heard before? Maybe so, but it's the truth.

Proactively preventing fraud, investigating suspicions of fraud, stopping frauds in progress, and punishing those who commit ethical violations are integral elements of true fraud prevention. Employees are affected by how fraud is handled, so swiftly dealing with unethical behavior is critical to encouraging good behavior.

To discourage fraudulent behavior, a company must be clear about rules and expectations, and take action when fraud is committed. Management must emphasize the importance of internal controls and adherence to policies and procedures. Internal controls will be discussed in greater detail in later chapters.

Summary

Larger frauds are generally committed by those in higher positions within a company. A higher position brings with it more access to information, computer systems, people, and assets; therefore, the opportunity to commit fraud and cover it up is increased.

To help detect fraud, management and owners must be aware of the common personal red flags that may indicate that an employee is involved in a scheme to defraud the company. The clues lie in personal problems such as addictions, legal troubles, or a pattern of dishonest behavior. Unusual attitudes or behaviors at work can also raise suspicions, particularly when employees are uncooperative with others or overly possessive of job duties and documentation.

We may like to think of embezzlers and defrauders as horrible people completely devoid of morals and ethics. That's just simply not the case. Many of them are people who have shown themselves to be trustworthy throughout the years. By proving themselves to management, they have been given increased responsibility and have been entrusted with assets and information.

How, then, do people end up committing fraud? And how do they steal from the very people who have placed trust in them, namely owners, shareholders, boards of directors, and management? It goes back to that triangle of fraud, which includes motive, opportunity, and rationalization. When the opportunity arises and the thief has a need or desire, along with a justification for the fraud, the theft will happen.

Notes

1. 2006 Report to the Nation, Association of Certified Fraud Examiners, Austin, TX.
2. Ibid.
3. 2004 Report to the Nation, Association of Certified Fraud Examiners, Austin, TX.
4. 2002 Report to the Nation, Association of Certified Fraud Examiners, Austin, TX.
5. 2006 Report to the Nation, Association of Certified Fraud Examiners, Austin, TX.
6. Ibid.
7. Ibid.
8. 2006 Report to the Nation, Association of Certified Fraud Examiners, Austin, TX.
9. 2006 Fraud Survey by KPMG, an Australian partnership and a member firm of the KPMG network of independent member firms affiliated with KPMG International, a Swiss cooperative.

CHAPTER 3

Red Flags of Fraud

After reading this chapter, you will be able to

- Recognize structural and operational defects that make companies susceptible to internal fraud.

- Learn personnel practices that may increase the likelihood of fraud committed by employees.

- Identify some of the most common red flags of fraud as they relate to a company's accounting system and financial performance.

We have already discussed a number of warning signs in individuals that might lead management to consider whether an employee is committing fraud against the company. This chapter examines characteristics of companies and their operations that might give rise to suspicions of fraud.

There can be fraud warning signs in a company's structure or operations. Some companies are set up in a way that increases their risk of internal fraud. Furthermore, a company may have certain operational characteristics that can put it at greater risk of fraud.

Finally, there may be signs that fraud is actually occurring. These indicators of fraudulent activity can be as simple as questionable documentation or as complex as an unusual relationship between employees. Such signs must be evaluated to determine whether they have legitimate explanations or whether fraud may actually be occurring. More often than not, the evaluation will end with a conclusion that nothing was amiss. This is okay. The important point is that an evaluation was made and there was an opportunity to detect fraud if it was indeed occurring.

Many indicators of fraudulent activity come to light through the accounting process. Ideally, companies have policies and procedures in place to prevent errors and fraud from occurring and to alert management when problems arise. However, companies don't always have processes in place to detect or prevent fraud, which is why additional fraud prevention measures are discussed in subsequent chapters.

Structural Red Flags

A company's setup and division of duties can create opportunities for fraud, and employees who are familiar with the operations and the processes can exploit these weaknesses. Companies have to trust their employees to carry out job duties, oversee data and assets, and protect the company's interests, but it is that trust that gives rise to fraud opportunities.

When evaluating a company's structure and system for fraud, it is important to note that the company's culture dictates behavior to a large extent. A company that only pays lip service to ethical behavior is more likely to experience fraud problems than a company that has a strong policy on ethics that is adhered to and enforced. Ethical behavior toward employees, customers, vendors, and shareholders should be both emphasized and exhibited.

It is especially important for senior management to model the behavior that employees are expected to exhibit. If management is openly dishonest and deceitful, this example may easily work its way through the ranks. Employees can be expected to behave ethically only if their managers and executives are manifestly ethical as well.

The relationships that may develop between employees and people who do business with a company are impossible to prevent. It is a simple fact that a purchasing agent who has worked with a particular vendor for years may have developed a friendship. It is these personal relationships that can facilitate fraud. As we've learned, collusion between employees dramatically increases the length of time a fraud scheme will go on as well as the dollar losses experienced by the company. Experts suggest that job rotation can cut down on the possibility of fraud that stems from these personal relationships, inasmuch as job rotation disrupts those personal connections. What may be lost in terms of good will because of a working relationship between the purchasing agent and the vendor can be more than made up through a decreased fraud risk.

Companies without good educational programs in place may be at a greater risk of fraud. First, a company should provide proper training so employees can learn their job duties. If employees are not adequately trained, they may fail to perform their duties properly. Fraud may be one way to cover up this on-the-job failure. Second, good educational programs also include training about fraud and about ethical policies at the company. Employees must be educated about the ethical behavior expected of them if they are going to act ethically.

Ethical policies are of no use to a company if they are not enforced. When ethical violations are discovered, it is important to punish the offenders appropriately. Punishment for fraudulent activities could range from a verbal reprimand to termination and legal action. Whatever the punishment, it must be doled out in proportion to the act committed. Rules must be enforced consistently and fairly in order for them to have a deterrent effect on would-be thieves.

The physical security of the company's premises and its assets plays an important role in the prevention of internal fraud. Not only does it directly prevent the theft and abuse of physical assets, it indirectly protects the company in other ways. Visible physical security sends a message to employees about how management secures the company in general. Conversely, lax physical security might inadvertently send employees the message that the company is not diligently monitoring its information, assets, and valuables.

Good security should also include restricted access to computers and data. It's easy to consider the need for security guards and locked doors, but access to digital information must also be secured. Many employees and managers don't think about the security of the computer system because they don't fully understand how the systems work anyway. But the fact remains that computer systems must be secured in such a way that employees are able to access only the information that they need. Access to unnecessary data and processes can give way to acts of fraud and opportunities to cover up the fraud.

Good fraud prevention depends on the presence and enforcement of good internal controls, which include both policies and procedures designed to protect the company, its assets, and the integrity of its financial data. When companies lack good internal controls or they choose not to enforce the rules, they create opportunities for employees to commit fraud. When employees know that the rules will not be enforced and that fraud will not result in punishment, the likelihood that fraud will occur is greater.

Personnel Red Flags

Employee screening and monitoring policies and procedures play an important role in preventing and detecting fraud, and so do the rules and restrictions placed on employees.

Although most employees who commit fraud have no prior record of fraud-related charges or convictions, that doesn't mean personnel screening procedures should be scrapped altogether. Because reasonable background checks and verifications can weed out some higher-risk employees, they are key components of fraud prevention. Furthermore, once employees are on board, they must have a clear understanding of the policies they will be required to follow. Companies that are lax in communicating clear expectations about ethical behavior and adherence to the code of conduct are creating an environment in which fraud may be more likely to occur.

Adequate staffing is a necessary component of fraud prevention, whether management accepts it or not. Understaffing can cause burdensome workloads, and employees who aren't completing work or meeting expectations might turn to fraud as a quick fix. Staff burdened under unrealistic work loads should be viewed as potential fraudsters, and steps must be taken to correct this deficiency.

Proper training of employees is an important part of fraud prevention. Employees should certainly be trained about fraud and its warning signs, as well as about the company's ethics policy. But it is also important to sufficiently train an employee regarding her or his job duties and responsibilities. Employees who can't perform their jobs might resort to fraud to make up for their incompetence. Proper training in this regard can help avoid such a risk.

Procedurally, accurate personnel records should be maintained as they relate to dishonest behavior and disciplinary actions. Companies that do not do so are at greater risk of fraud, because there will not be enough information available when employees are being considered for job transfers or promotions. For example, an employee with undocumented unethical workplace behavior might inadvertently get promoted to a job that involves money-handling duties. With documentation of the prior behavior, management will have the necessary information to deny that particular promotion.

How the employees are managed plays an important part in the likelihood that a company will experience internal fraud. Employees react definitively to the company's management style. Domineering, overbearing managers and executives can create discord and disloyalty. However, executives who are too hands-off may also encourage fraud and bad behavior because of a lack of oversight and monitoring. There is a fine balance that must be achieved in managing employees to keep from creating an environment that inadvertently encourages fraud.

Treating employees fairly and paying them at market wage rates can help prevent fraud too. One common justification for theft from a business is that an employee felt underpaid. This can be mitigated by being aware of pay rates at other companies for similar positions. Employees who feel valued and properly compensated are less likely to feel entitled to steal.

An employee may also justify a theft when she or he feels unfairly treated. It is easy to justify by rationalizing that the employee is just "getting back" at the company for all the wrongs she or he had to endure. Again, companies should attempt to be swift but fair in administration and discipline to help guard against this justification of theft.

Strained relationships between employees can indicate a fraud problem. This is especially evident if several employees from one area of the company leave at the same time. This can indicate that a supervisor is acting unethically or asking employees to do so, or both. At the very least, mass departures indicate a management problem in that area of the company. At worst, it suggests that something illegal or unethical is occurring, something that needs to be examined.

Closely related to this is the problem of low employee morale and low job satisfaction. Granted, there may always be some unhappy employees, but when this is a pervasive problem in a department or an area of the company, it merits further investigation. Low motivation on the part of employees might indicate that the company simply has a bad manager or supervisor. However, it could indicate a fraud problem, so these things must be looked into.

Turnover in key positions in a company is also something that should be examined. Although turnover can occur for various reasons, possible indicators of fraud include unusual frequency or particular positions being vacated. The departure of key personnel with finance positions is worthy of further investigation.

Operational Red Flags

One of the key red flags of fraud within a company is operating in "crisis mode" or "fire drill mode" on an ongoing basis. This is particularly dangerous because no one within the company ever has a chance to see what "normal" operations look like. How would an employee ever be able to flag something as unusual when all operations are frenzied? It's hard to pay attention to details when employees are running a race that never ends.

It's also dangerous for a company to operate without clear lines of authority. If an employee is unclear about who manages what area or who should receive complaints, that employee is less likely to report suspicious behavior. It is imperative that all employees know who their direct supervisor is, and who that person's direct supervisor is, and so on. The "pecking order" must be clear; that way, employees who witness potentially unethical behavior know whom to approach next.

Some companies run well with a "team" concept throughout, but still the teams always know who ranks above them in the chain of authority if trouble should arise. Even though individual team members may be empowered to make more decisions than employees who work under a more traditional operating structure, fraud can still be prevented and reported if clear lines of authority are drawn.

A common problem, particularly in smaller companies, is the lack of segregation of duties. Segregation of duties is one of the most basic internal control concepts in the accounting function. Simply put, duties surrounding certain areas of the accounting process should be divided so that one person does not have too much control over or access to the entire area.

For example, a person depositing money in the bank should not be responsible for updating customer accounts; that person might steal from the deposit and then conceal it by making fraudulent entries to customer accounts. Dividing the duties of depositing and updating accounts makes it more likely that a theft from the deposit could be both prevented and discovered.

In small companies, it is sometimes difficult to have proper segregation of duties because there just aren't enough people to divide the tasks among. However, most often that is just an excuse. A company committed to proper segregation of duties could have controls in place with the help of management and owners. Even a small group of three employees could have a reasonably effective segregation of duties to prevent fraud.

Companies with lax rules regarding authorization of transactions have a higher risk of internal fraud. A company should have controls in place to allow employees only certain predetermined levels of authority, and there should also be a process for monitoring the authorization levels to determine the level of compliance.

Management should be on the lookout for employees who fail to receive proper authorization, or for employees who do things to get around the controls. For example, if an employee is authorized to spend up to $10,000 without prior approval but has two expenditures of $6,000 each ($12,000 total) for the same vendor in a short period of time, this should be questioned. Was this one $12,000 project that was broken into two pieces to circumvent the authorization process? If the answer is yes, management should look for additional instances of such behavior and should take corrective action.

A lack of internal controls in general is one of the most significant operational red flags a company can exhibit. Policies and procedures that protect the integrity of the accounting and finance function are essential for a company to have low internal fraud. Of course, when there are few or even no controls in place, employees are free to engage in behavior that harms the company, and it may go completely undetected.

Almost as bad as the absence of internal controls is the unwillingness to correct deficient controls. Improvements can always be made, especially in areas with higher levels of fraud risk. Management's unwillingness to improve internal controls or change procedures to reflect newer risks creates a major red flag for fraud.

IN THE REAL WORLD

Failure to Reconcile Accounts

A small manufacturer was acquired by an investor group that did not examine inventory on taking over. The accounting manager was stealing cash and balancing the books by making numerous accounting entries to the purchasing and inventory system. He was aware that management didn't know whether the inventory

Accounting System Red Flags

The lack of adequate internal controls is both an organizational problem and an accounting system red flag. A good, secure accounting system cannot exist without internal controls. The controls are the checks and balances that ensure transactions are authorized, completed, and recorded properly. Even if no employees are committing fraud, it is next to impossible for the company to have accounting records that are free from error if there are no controls.

It is especially troublesome when weaknesses in the internal controls are pointed out by auditors and consultants and they are not subsequently corrected or improved. The longer employees are on the job, the more familiar they become with these weaknesses and the easier it is to exploit them.

Poor accounting records in general are also a red flag of fraud. For one thing, poor recordkeeping systems encourage fraud because employees know that information is not being properly recorded and evidence of fraud may be easy to conceal. In addition, poor accounting records may actually be a symptom of fraud that is occurring. It can be difficult to keep good records when time is being spent on a fraud scheme, or the records may have deteriorated because an employee doesn't know how to keep them from looking suspicious when committing fraud. Either way, as a cause or an effect of fraud, poor accounting records are a concern.

TIPS AND TECHNIQUES

Documentation Red Flags

- Missing or altered documents
- Evidence of backdating documents
- No original documents available
- Documents that directly conflict with one another
- Questionable signatures on documents

Naturally, discrepancies in a company's accounting records are often a red flag of fraud. The key is being able to distinguish between normal errors in the records and true red flags of fraud. Fortunately, many questionable items can be cleared up rather quickly if they are simply the result of an error in the system or an error committed by a user of the system. Documentation can solve the mystery if it's just an error. It is those unexplained "errors" that are troublesome.

A quick look at a company's financial statements may reveal that certain account balances are the opposite of a normal ending balance. For example, an accounts payable account shows a debit balance instead of a credit balance. (Some might say that this is a "negative" accounts payable.) An examination of the account details might quickly reveal a bill incorrectly entered into the system or an equally simple explanation. However, when the source of an obvious error like this cannot be found, questions about fraud should be raised.

A simple analytical review of income statement and balance sheet accounts might reveal some interesting information about the financial statements. Accounts should be compared from period to period, noting dollar differences and percentage changes. Again, there may be some simple explanations for any significant variances. When the variances can't be explained, that is when a red flag goes up.

Transactions that are not recorded in a timely manner can be suspicious, as can be the lack of timeliness in reconciling accounts. Accounting entries made at the end of an accounting period can be perfectly normal, given that employees are completing reconciliations and making adjustment entries. However, management should be on the lookout for entries at the end of a period that significantly affect the company's financial results for the period. An unusual application of accounting rules is also a red flag, all the more suspicious when that unusual application enhances the company's financial position.

Take for example a company that typically capitalizes a certain cost and has a set schedule for expensing that cost. All of a sudden, management decides to increase the length of time over which the cost is expensed, effectively decreasing the expense amount for each accounting period. If there is no substantive change in the circumstances under which this cost is incurred and no change in the accounting rules, this would appear to be unusual. It is especially unusual because the new treatment (without any identifiable justification) will make the financial results for this period look better. That is quite apparently a red flag of fraud.

There are hundreds and possibly thousands of things that could be considered red flags of fraud when the details of accounting transactions are examined. Some of the basic red flags—no matter the account in which a transaction is booked—include

- **Unusual timing of the transaction.** This includes the time of day, the day of the week, or the season.

- **Frequency of transactions.** Transactions that are occurring too frequently or not frequently enough are suspicious. Each company has its own operating patterns, and the transactions should be booked accordingly.

- **Unusual amounts recorded.** Take notice of whether an account has many large, round numbers entered. Consider whether some of the transactions in the account are far too large or far too small.

- **Questionable parties involved.** Should the company be paying an outside party? Is a payment being made to a related party? Is the company paying large sums to a vendor whose name is not easily recognizable?

TIPS AND TECHNIQUES

Accounting System Red Flags: Cash Receipts

- Cash and checks not properly secured
- Infrequent bank deposits

TIPS AND TECHNIQUES (CONTINUED)

- Missing or voided receipts
- Duties of receiving cash and posting to accounts not segregated
- Duties of preparation of deposit and issuing receipts not segregated
- Large, recurring fluctuations in bank account balances
- Excessive voided transactions without explanations
- Delay in reconciling bank accounts
- Insufficient supervision of cash receipts process

TIPS AND TECHNIQUES

Accounting System Red Flags: Accounts Receivable

- Lack of policies regarding write-offs
- No supervision or review of write-offs
- Duties of posting to accounts and receiving cash not segregated
- Frequent undocumented or unapproved adjustments, credits, and write-offs
- Dramatic increase in allowance for doubtful accounts, even related financial statement accounts are changing for the better
- Reluctance to reserve for or write off accounts receivable
- Accounts receivable increasing or decreasing in a way not in accord with changing sales figures
- Unexplained deterioration in the collection cycle

TIPS AND TECHNIQUES

Accounting System Red Flags: Accounts Payable

- Recurring identical amounts from the same vendor
- Multiple vendors with similar names in the accounting systems
- Multiple addresses for the same vendor
- Discrepancies between vendor addresses on checks and those in the vendor master file
- Lack of documentation for changes to vendor master files
- Sequential invoice numbers from the same vendor
- Payments to a vendor increasing dramatically for no apparent reason
- Duties of check preparation and posting to vendor accounts not segregated
- Excessive credit adjustments for a particular vendor
- Pattern of adjustments to accounts payable for goods returned
- Manually prepared disbursement checks
- Vendor payments booked directly to expense account instead of accounts payable

Financial Performance Red Flags

When a company creates unrealistic performance measures for individuals or the company as a whole, management can be set up for disaster. Aggressive performance measures may seem like good goal-setting tactics, but the unfortunate truth is that when people can't meet those goals, they may turn to fraud. When a company's financial statements, financial performance, and financial position are examined, a number of red flags may indicate the presence of fraud.

Companies that are outpacing competitors in the same industry merit additional scrutiny. Surely there is always an industry leader, and someone must be the best. However, there are times when a company's industry-leading numbers are suspect. For example, a company that has never been terribly successful and that hasn't made significant changes in management or operations probably won't legitimately jump to the front of the pack.

A company that is having tremendous success when the rest of the industry in depressed may also need to be examined closely. It is plausible that a company has an advantage in an industry due to operating efficiencies, intellectual property, or other positive attributes. But it is also possible that a company enjoying success during an industry downturn may be inflating sales figures and underreporting expenses.

The case of WorldCom illustrates another problem in dissecting financial statements and financial performance. A company that is continuously acquiring companies and changing its core business is next to impossible to analyze in a historical context. There is often no way for an outsider to effectively segregate pieces of a company's business to make a meaningful comparison of financials from year to year. WorldCom was acquiring companies and segments of businesses rapidly, and users of the financial statements couldn't get a handle on what "normal" operations really were and how the financials for those operations should look.

Outpacing Competitors

WorldCom may be one of the most recognizable examples of a company outpacing competitors. The stock price rose rapidly because the company was doing well on paper. Competitors in the telecommunications industry were doing well in the late 1990s, but WorldCom was doing even better. This should have raised a huge red flag for every user of the company's financial statements. How was WorldCom able to achieve such outstanding numbers as compared with the rest of the industry?

Further complicating the situation was that the company was constantly in "deal mode." Operations could almost never be compared with those of a prior period, because the prior period didn't include the most recent acquisitions. As the company acquired other businesses at a breakneck pace, the accounting systems and the company's accountability could not keep up.

In the end, the financial results reported by WorldCom were fictional, and income restatements totaled in the billions.

Companies with insufficient working capital or high debt loads are sometimes at a higher risk of fraud. In addition to normal pressure on the company and its executives to perform well, the lack of working capital and a high debt load make good performance harder. Limited access to cash or restrictive loan agreements may create a situation in which fraud helps in meeting goals.

Ratio analysis may be helpful in analyzing a company's financial situation. Comparing the ratios across quarters and years can yield some interesting information about operations, and it might point to areas of the company that should be examined for evidence of fraud. Ratios might also be compared with industry benchmarks or the ratios of other companies in the same industry. These comparisons could uncover, for example, sales growing much faster than normal for the industry or a high level of accounts receivable to sales. Ratios aren't evidence of fraud by themselves, but they can yield interesting information about a company's operations.

Companies feeling a profit squeeze may be at a higher risk for fraud. When expenses are rising faster than revenues or when expenses are eating up a greater percentage of the budget, fraud may be more likely to occur. Difficult business conditions can trigger fraud. Additionally, the presence of rising costs may indicate that a fraud is in process and is being buried in the operating expenses, causing them to be higher than normal.

When companies are reporting significant increases in revenue, other accounts normally should show increases too. Accounts that often increase in relation to sales increases include inventory on hand and accounts receivable. It is only natural that these accounts should increase if there are legitimate increases in revenue. When they do not increase, the revenue figures should be examined very carefully.

One common red flag of fraud is a consistent cash crunch even when revenues are reported to be continuously growing. It makes sense that higher sales may create a temporary cash shortage while the company is spending money on materials and production and waiting to be paid by customers. However, a consistent cash flow problem period after period, even when the profit and loss statement shows progress, is troubling.

This was one of the many warning signs at Enron. The company was reporting excellent revenues period after period, but never seemed to have any cash to show for the sales. As it turned out, much of the revenue stream was phony, created by improperly recognizing revenue early and recognizing related-party transactions as revenue when they should not have been. The sales figures weren't really sales at all, and the result was that the company didn't have any cash to show for it.

Finally, audit results should be examined for indicators of internal fraud. In particular, a pattern of similar proposed audit adjustments year after year could signal a problem. Even if repeated adjustments are deemed immaterial to the financial statements, their cumulative effect on the financial statements should be examined, and the circumstances causing the repetitive problems should be investigated.

TIPS AND TECHNIQUES

Financial Performance Red Flags

- Doing business in a volatile industry
- High concentration of business with a small number of customers
- Rapid expansion, especially when not planned well
- Deterioration in the quality of earnings over time
- Company involved in significant litigation
- Reduction in sales backlogs, indicating lower future sales

Professional Service Red Flags

Companies with frequent or unusual changes in auditors, attorneys, or banks merit additional scrutiny. One such problem is using multiple firms or companies for services. Using more than one company is not, in and of itself, a warning sign of fraud. However, it does become suspicious when it seems that a company is using multiple firms so that no one firm ever gets a complete picture of the company's situation.

For example, companies often use more than one law firm when particular areas of expertise are required. For example, one law firm may be hired specifically to handle intellectual property issues, while another law firm is hired to handle all general legal matters. However, it is questionable when a company is using multiple firms for general legal matters or similar types of cases. Why would the company need to use more than one law firm for similar legal matters? Suspicions should be raised when there is no substantive reason for using more than one firm or when the firms chosen appear to duplicate one another's efforts in certain areas.

Firm-hopping is also cause for concern. In terms of the outside accountants and auditors, frequent switching may suggest disagreements about material financial issues. The auditors may have required certain audit procedures or disclosures to be implemented, and the company may have refused. Frequent changes in attorneys may be equally as troubling, and the reasons for the changes should be questioned.

Using several banks can be a red flag of fraud as well. Although it may be normal to have several bank accounts, when a company uses several banks simultaneously, none of the banks has a full picture of the company's financial situation. Using multiple banks also increases fraud risk, because it is easier for a rogue employee to create or use a bank account improperly without being noticed. It's not unheard of for management to lose track of a bank account, which is later used by an employee to embezzle funds.

On a related note, how management interacts with its professional service providers is also important. Companies that are reluctant to share information with their auditors and attorneys should be carefully watched. The company should be volunteering details of relevant legal and financial situations. Certainly in response to requests for additional information and documentation, management should be forthcoming and cooperative.

When management denies auditors or examiners access to personnel, customers, vendors, documents, or other professional service providers, it is very alarming. Records and facilities should be easily accessible, especially if the access is tied to risky areas of the financial statements. For example, inventory is a much-abused line item on the financial statements. Management should allow auditors full access to inventory records and physical inventory at any and all locations. Any denial of or delay in granting access should be viewed as a huge red flag of fraud.

Aggressive deadlines or demands by management in regard to the resolution of complex issues may signal a problem. It is only natural that accountants, auditors, and attorneys would need ample time to dissect an issue and give a proper opinion. A "rush job" on such things might signal an attempt by management to force professionals to do a less than thorough analysis of the situation.

Summary

Structural deficiencies within a company can lead to a greater instance of occupational fraud. In order to avoid a structure that encourages fraud, management must evaluate the lines of authority and the division of duties among employees.

Precautions must be taken to prevent collusion between employees and between employees and outside parties. Being aware of the potential for fraud involves having a finger on the pulse of employees. Owners and executives need to constantly evaluate the relationships between employees and the way employees perceive management.

Fraud prevention also relies heavily on good control procedures, ethics policies that are enforced, and modeling of ethical behavior by senior management. Personnel must be screened and evaluated for high-risk attributes, and management must adequately supervise employees to detect any ongoing red flags of fraud.

Accounting records and financial statements must be regularly examined for the presence of red flags of fraud. Performance goals for individuals, departments, operating units, and the company as a whole must be reasonable and attainable; if they are not, incentives to commit fraud may exist. Actual financial performance should be examined in relation to industry benchmarks and competitor performance. Financial statement ratios can provide valuable information about a company's financial performance as well as areas at risk for fraud.

One of the keys to detecting fraud is the consistent monitoring of employees, operations, and financials for the presence of things that are unusual.

CHAPTER 4

Asset Misappropriation, Bribery, and Corruption

After reading this chapter, you will be able to

- Identify common asset misappropriation schemes and their warning signs.
- Detect and prevent asset misappropriation schemes to limit losses to the organization.

- Recognize the warning signs of bribery and corruption, and identify critical items to examine for evidence of bribery and corruption.

- Understand procedures that may help prevent bribery and corruption schemes.

The most commonly occurring fraud within corporations is asset misappropriation. According to the Association of Certified Fraud Examiners, more than 91% of all internal fraud schemes involved an asset misappropriation element, and the median loss from an asset misappropriation was $150,000.[1] Asset misappropriations include the misuse or theft of assets belonging to a company.

These are the white collar crimes we think about most, probably because they are so commonplace in terms of the number of cases that occur. Furthermore, they are the kinds of cases we most commonly hear about in the press.

By comparison, bribery and corruption schemes occur far less frequently, with 31% of fraud schemes including this element.[2] Yet these schemes are far more costly on a per-incident basis, with a median cost of $538,000 per fraud.[3] Such schemes include the use of one's position or power to influence a transaction, and more specifically these schemes could involve bribery, kickbacks, or conflicts of interest.

Asset Misappropriation Schemes

Asset misappropriations can be divided between cash schemes and non–cash schemes. Cash schemes simply involve the theft of money via checks, money orders, or paper currency; they can be further divided between schemes focusing on cash receipts and those related to cash disbursements. Non-cash schemes involve all other thefts of assets, such as inventory, equipment, supplies, or information. Cash theft is present in almost 88% of asset misappropriations schemes, and non-cash theft is present in 23% of cases, with *both* cash and non-cash theft present in some fraud schemes.[4]

Cash Receipts

Currency is easy to steal because it often comes with no paper trail. Receipts help control this somewhat, but many thieves can devise ways around receipts. In organizations that don't use receipts, the cash is at even greater risk of theft.

But cash fraud schemes aren't limited to the theft of actual currency on hand. Most of the time, cash is stolen through schemes involving checks or other financial instruments. These frauds are more difficult to carry out because the thief has to find a way to forge a signature, divert a check, or otherwise manipulate the systems within an organization.

The theft of cash, either as check or as currency, can occur in two ways. There can be skimming, which is the taking of funds before they are ever recorded on the books of the company. For example, this may include taking customer payments for services that haven't yet been recorded as sales on the books. Cash larceny, on the other hand, involves the theft of funds after there has been a transaction recorded. For example, cash larceny occurs when an employee steals a customer check that was sent as a payment on account. Because the account already has record of a sale and an expected payment, this theft falls under larceny.

Cash Receipts Fraud

A large church suffered a significant cash fraud at the hands of an unscrupulous bookkeeper. Controls were in place to guard against theft. A group of volunteers counted the weekly cash collections together, overseeing one another. A sheet documenting the cash collections was prepared and submitted to the bookkeeper along with the cash.

The bookkeeper never deposited the cash, but kept the documentation in the church's files. The documentation was never compared against the bank deposits, so for more than two years, the bookkeeper stole nearly all cash collections without detection.

The fraud was detected when the bookkeeper took a sick day and another employee received the bank statement. Although she did not normally look at the bank statements, the envelope was already open so she decided to examine the contents. She immediately found checks made payable to the bookkeeper. An investigation ensued, and the larger theft of cash was quickly uncovered.

Cash Receipts Schemes: Skimming

Cash skimming is harder to detect than cash larceny, because it involves at least some element of unrecorded transactions. For example, suppose a customer enters a business to make a purchase with currency. The sale of a product and the currency don't exist for the company until some sort of record is created. Typically, this would happen when the purchase entered into the cash register. If the employee steals the cash prior to recording anything regarding the sale or payment, the employee has skimmed.

A common cash-skimming scheme involves unrecorded sales, whereby an employee sells items and receives payment but records neither the sale nor the payment—and personally keeps the proceeds. Another skimming scheme involves theft of cash or checks from customer payments, with the dishonest employee taking them as they come into the company but before they can be recorded as received.

Skimming cash seems easy enough to pull off, but still some work must be done to conceal the theft. If the theft is not concealed, later problems such as missing inventory or a customer complaint about an account balance may reveal the fraud. Schemes such as these are usually concealed by using some sort of write-off or credit to force the accounts to balance.

A more complicated way to conceal the theft of a customer payment is through lapping. In a lapping scheme, an employee steals a customer's payment and applies later payments by other customers to make the first customer's account balance. This type of scheme can get complicated very quickly, because each time the thief corrects one account, it leaves one or two new accounts out of balance, and they must eventually be corrected as well.

Cash Receipts Schemes: Larceny

Cash larceny occurs when cash has been received, has been recorded on the company's books in some fashion, and then is later stolen. Suppose that the customer comes into the business and pays with cash but also requests a written receipt. The company has a record of that cash payment, and if an employee tries to steal it, the employee would be committing larceny.

Cash larceny can be committed in several ways. One common way is through theft of the bank deposit, whereby the employee takes funds out of the deposit before it goes to the bank. This is more complicated than skimming, because in this situation, a record has already been created regarding the deposit.

Most often, additional work needs to be done to cover the theft; deposit lapping is one option. In this scheme, funds from later deposits are used to supplement the earlier deposit from which funds were stolen. This way, when the original deposit finally goes to the bank, the total deposit will match the company's accounting records. This, too, can get complicated quickly, and may require the employee to keep lots of notes.

Cash Disbursements

The next general category of cash misappropriations is referred to as fraudulent disbursements. Fraudulent disbursements occur when an employee causes an organization to pay money under false pretenses. One of the most common ways that this can happen is through check tampering, in which an employee may forge or alter a check for her or his own benefit. The employee may also steal a legitimate check and forge the endorsement to benefit from the funds. More modern methods of committing fraudulent disbursements include false wire transfers or electronic transfers, or fraudulent credit card transactions.

Billing schemes are another way of accomplishing a cash disbursement fraud. One of the simplest billing schemes involves a vendor inflating an invoice to a company. The inflated invoice may include billings for items not ordered by the company, items not received by the company, or inflated prices.

A second straightforward way to advance a billing scheme is by causing a company to pay for an employee's personal expenses. Personal charges may be put on a company credit card that is paid with company funds. A personal credit card could also be used for the personal expenses, and the company may pay that bill or pay the employee directly. Other schemes include billing the company for goods and services received by the employee for personal purposes.

IN THE REAL WORLD

Cash Disbursement Fraud

A company's bookkeeper was responsible for preparing checks to pay the company's bills. The checks and the associated invoices were presented to the check signer, who would briefly examine the invoices and sign the checks.

One day the check signer decided that reviewing invoices was too much trouble, so he signed a stack of blank checks for the bookkeeper to use for bill payments. The first thing she did was to get a credit card from the same issuer the company used. She paid her bill with company checks. If anyone later examined the checks, they would see a check payable to the known credit card company and would likely think nothing of it. The scheme was successful for more than two years, and was eventually discovered only by accident.

A more complicated cash disbursement scheme involves setting up a shell company. Here, the employee defrauds the company by setting up a fake company (a "shell" company) to provide goods and services to the company. The fake company often provides no goods or services, but bills the victim company and receives payments. Other times, the fake company acts as a pass-through for legitimate goods and services but inflates the prices that are billed to the victim company.

IN THE REAL WORLD

Shell Companies

The purchasing manager of a high-tech company had a close working relationship with a few key suppliers of computer components. He devised a scheme to create a shell company in collusion with his contacts at the suppliers. The shell company procured the goods needed by the high-tech company and sold them to the company at artificially high prices. The purchasing manager and his conspirators split the proceeds from this shell company scheme. Over a period of several years, the company paid millions of dollars more than it should have for the components. The purchasing agent pocketed hundreds of thousands of dollars from his portion of the profits from the shell company.

There are a number of ways to manipulate legitimate vendors, and one of them is through a pay-and-return scheme. A dishonest employee causes the company to overpay a vendor, and then the vendor is contacted and asked to return the overpayment. The dishonest employee devises a way to personally receive and keep that overpayment.

Manipulation of the payroll system is yet another means by which a cash disbursement scheme can be carried out. The schemes can include ghost employees, falsified hours, inflated pay rates, understated leave and vacation time, and unauthorized bonuses and commissions. All of these are designed to cause the victim company to pay money or give benefits that are not really due to the recipient.

Non-Cash Fraud

Non-cash frauds are aimed at stealing anything the company owns other than cash or cash equivalents. This might be the theft of inventory, supplies, fixed assets, or other hard assets owned by the company. Some of these items are easy to steal simply because of a lack of management oversight. Items in areas with low foot traffic might be easy to steal because the theft may not be noticed for a period of time. Lax monitoring and security may also make hard assets fairly easy to steal at some companies.

The theft of inventory can be covered up by falsifying receiving records. An employee may steal items from an incoming shipment and then falsify a receiving report to indicate that the missing items were never received or were received but defective. This is typically only a temporary solution to the problem, as the theft may come to light when the vendor invoice is received and compared with receiving documents.

Another way to conceal the theft of merchandise is through false sales orders or shipping documents. These items may explain the missing inventory, but the fraud is subject to discovery when a customer fails to pay for the sale or return the merchandise. This scheme requires a follow-up act to destroy documentation or cancel a sale in the system.

Company assets can also be stolen via a fraudulent write-off. A dishonest employee can write off assets or inventory as scrap, junk, obsolete, or destroyed, and then appropriate the asset for herself or himself with little chance of detection.

Detecting Asset Misappropriation

The most effective way to discover cash fraud schemes within companies is through monitoring of employees. This doesn't necessarily mean direct monitoring by supervisors or managers. It could also be accomplished through proper segregation of duties whereby employees naturally are checking one another's work.

Internal cash thefts can be discovered by monitoring write-off accounts. Accounts that are used for customer credits, write-off of balances, or other reconciling or adjusting items are ripe for abuse. They are often not monitored carefully, and there are often a high number of small transactions flowing through them. Management should also be monitoring transactions such as "voids," which may increase in frequency when a fraud scheme is being perpetrated. Unusually high shrinkage in inventory may also tip management off to theft.

The analysis of ratios and trends can be invaluable in detecting asset misappropriations. Specifically, accounts should be analyzed for higher-than-normal ratios related to accounts receivable write-offs, credits, inventory obsolescence, warranty costs, rebates, and sales returns. Management should also watch for declining gross profit margins, which could signal unrecorded sales.

Detecting shell company schemes can be difficult. It often involves the analysis of vendor data, looking for unusual billing addresses, company names, and check endorsements. Management must also compare invoices against actual goods and services received to detect discrepancies in the data. Unfortunately, employees who mastermind these schemes often have the ability to manipulate systems so that an analysis of goods and services received may not show a discrepancy. Shell-company schemes often involve multiple employees and outside parties. This collusion makes the fraud even more difficult to detect. A company may have good internal controls, but collusion can easily nullify them.

Software programs can analyze accounting system data to detect anomalies. Such software looks for unusual amounts and other suspicious data and can analyze a significant amount of data in a very short period of time. Computer programs can also compare vendor data such as addresses and phone numbers with employee data to search for any duplicate information that may signal an inappropriate relationship.

Some data is best analyzed by human beings who are familiar with the company's operations, vendors, and accounting system. They can look for unknown vendors, inappropriate pricing levels, goods or services that appear unusual, excessive purchases of services, and other such unusual characteristics.

Careful review of inventory and fixed asset records are necessary to detect fraud. In particular, the details of write-off accounts and adjusting entries must be carefully examined for irregularities. Shipping documents should be matched with sales and vice versa. Inventory write-offs should be supported with documentation authorizing the removal of scrapped or spoiled items.

TIPS AND TECHNIQUES

Detecting Asset Misappropriation: Accounts to Monitor

- Customer credits or write-offs
- Adjustment accounts
- Inventory scrap, spoilage, obsolescence
- Inventory shrinkage
- Fixed asset write-offs

Preventing Asset Misappropriation

As with detecting asset misappropriation schemes, monitoring employees is probably the single best way to prevent the schemes. Proper segregation of duties ensures that employees are checking and monitoring one another's work. Also, proper segregation doesn't allow any one employee to have too much control over the process. That means that if an accounting clerk has access to customer payments she may be able to steal them. But if someone else updates customer accounts, the first employee will be found out rather quickly.

Segregation of duties is also effective in preventing cash disbursement frauds, such as payroll schemes. It is one of the most common fraud prevention techniques and can be implemented relatively easily and cost effectively.

Examination of documentation can prevent both cash receipts and cash disbursement schemes. In part, employees may be deterred from committing fraud when they are aware that documentation is being examined regularly. The other reason document examination is effective is because of its actual results. An attempted fraud can be stopped when an astute employee compares documentation with products and services actually received.

Although it may sound archaic, the examination of checks themselves can yield important information. The front and back of the check should be examined, and the endorsement should be looked at carefully. Checks need to be examined for evidence of forged signatures, forged endorsements, and endorsement by inappropriate parties. Some banks no longer allow companies to receive their canceled checks with their bank statements, opting instead for providing digital images. This makes the examination of the checks more difficult, especially if the bank only provides only a copy of the front of each check.

Independent verification of accounts can help prevent and detect fraud related to both accounts receivable and the purchasing function. Customers and vendors should be contacted periodically and asked to verify account information. They can confirm the accuracy of billing and payment details. Any discrepancies with the company's records should be immediately investigated.

Surprise audits throughout the purchasing function can help to prevent disbursement schemes. It is advisable to examine accounts payable details, looking for overpayments, appropriate documentation, and approved vendors. These audits can be helpful even when no fraud is present, because they can uncover errors and inefficiencies in the process.

Companies should take action to prevent the possibility of collusion. This involves adopting procedures such as job rotation and vendor rotation. Employees should be rotated in order to disrupt relationships that may foster fraud and to uncover frauds in progress.

Physical security can help prevent asset misappropriation as well. Blank checks and critical documentation must be secured. Security cameras should monitor areas critical to the company's security and areas in which valuable assets may be stored.

TIPS AND TECHNIQUES

Techniques to Prevent Asset Misappropriation

- Employee monitoring
- Segregation of duties

TIPS AND TECHNIQUES (CONTINUED)

- Examination of documentation
- Examination of canceled checks
- Independent verification
- Surprise audits
- Job rotation
- Vendor rotation
- Physical security

Bribery and Corruption Schemes

When people think of bribery and corruption, many often think first of government involvement and politics. The reality is that bribery and corruption happen across all industries, including both the private and public sectors. These financial crimes can be some of the hardest to discover and prove. While other types of internal fraud usually have some sort of paper trail attached to them, many bribery and corruption schemes involve cash and do not have a paper trail. When a paper trail exists, it is often difficult to track down because much of the paper trail is outside of the company.

Bribery involves giving or receiving something of value in order to influence a transaction and ensure that something occurs in the future. For example, in a commercial transaction a bribe may be given in order to ensure that a certain contractor's bid is accepted. *Illegal gratuities*, in contrast, occur after a transaction has been completed.

Corruption schemes also include acts of *extortion*. Here, a perpetrator demands a sum of money or something of value with a threat of harm if the demands are not met. The harm could include physical harm, but could easily be the denial of a business contract or opportunity or the threat of actions to damage the reputation of a person or the company.

Conflicts of interest occur when an employee has an economic or other personal interest in a transaction. For example, an independent auditor should not own shares of stock in a company she or he is auditing. Another typical example of a conflict of interest occurs when a family member of an executive bids on a contract with the company. Clearly, the auditor or the executive may have a vested interest in the outcome of the business transaction, and that creates a conflict of interest.

Kickbacks are often received by an employee in a purchasing function. An outside vendor offers the purchasing agent a portion of the proceeds if a contract is awarded to the vendor. The vendor may be offering substandard products or services or may be charging a higher price than the rest of the market. Sometimes no products or services are rendered at all, but the purchasing agent sees to it that an invoice is still paid. The purchasing agent is receiving a payment for assisting the vendor in securing the contract or receiving payment, or both.

Corporate espionage is a fraud that is not as well-known as those mentioned previously. It includes the theft of trade secrets or other intellectual property, as well as copyright piracy. These schemes may not be discussed often, but they are costly to corporations, and it is in their best interest to be on the lookout for unscrupulous employees who may compromise the security of data and secrets.

Intellectual property can have significant value to companies; indeed for some companies, it can be the lifeblood of the organization.

High-tech companies in particular rely on their intellectual property such as patents and software code to continue operating. When those are compromised, a competitor may be given an unfair advantage.

There are many schemes that fall under the larger category of bribery and corruption, and they are often expensive and difficult to detect. As discussed further on in this chapter, companies must improve policies and procedures for management to have any hope of preventing and detecting schemes of these types.

Procurement Fraud

Procurement fraud is a subset of bribery and corruption schemes. It is essentially the manipulation of the process of obtaining a contract for goods and services. The manipulation is generally aimed at gaining an advantage in the bidding or proposal process, and the bad acts can range from the unfair use of insider information to the use of nefarious means to influence the process.

This type of fraud is often very difficult to detect. This is partly because companies are reluctant to admit that employees have been violating their fiduciary duties to the employer and partly because so much of the maneuvering happens outside the company's system of policies, procedures, and recordkeeping.

Procurement fraud can be broken down into three broad categories:

1. **Collusion between employees and vendors.** This can include kickbacks, bid rigging, gifts, or other enticements.

2. **Vendor fraud against a company.** A vendor may commit fraud against a company by substituting goods of inferior quality,

overcharging the company, or engaging in other false billing schemes.

3. **Collusion between multiple vendors.** Vendors may collude to artificially inflate the prices of goods and services in bids or proposals, or to help one another receive certain contracts based on agreements between them.

Company employees can collude with vendors to push contracts toward product or service providers that have a conflict of interest with the employee. For example, an employee's sibling may run a company bidding on a contract. If the employee funnels insider information toward the sibling, or if the employee gives the sibling other preferential treatment in the bidding and proposal process, a conflict of interest has unfairly influenced the process.

Common in the purchasing and receiving function is the payment of kickbacks or secret commissions, as discussed previously. The employee has a fiduciary duty to secure the best pricing for the company, but with a kickback scheme, the vendor is allowed to inflate the price to the company and the proceeds of that fraud are shared with the employee.

Vendors may also entice employees in a purchasing function to purchase more of a particular good or service than the company really needs. Some sort of kickback, commission, or gift may be given to the employee for buying in excess. Naturally, the company is harmed because it doesn't really need the additional goods or services; it is therefore spending too much money because of the bad acts of the purchasing agent.

Substitution of goods can be a costly and dangerous practice. Companies contract to receive a certain quality of goods or services within certain specifications. If the vendor substitutes lower-quality goods or services, the vendor instantly increases its profit margins. But the result for the company purchasing the goods can be dangerous.

A company relies on the receipt of a certain level of quality. The company is being cheated when inferior goods are secretly substituted, and the substitution may cause regulatory or safety problems. The company may require components that can withstand a certain level of heat, pressure, or other measures. A lower-quality part may be designed to withstand lower levels of those measurements and can ultimately be prone to higher failure rates.

Collusive bidding, also called bid rigging or price fixing, can be very damaging to the company that is purchasing goods and services from vendors. In bid rigging, vendors align themselves with one another to inflate the prices in the bids. While a company relies on a competitive bidding process to obtain the lowest price for certain goods or services, the bidders themselves are creating a situation in which the company essentially overpays for what it receives.

Detecting Bribery and Corruption

Cases of bribery and corruption are hard to detect, but the harm they cause to companies and organizations is undeniable. Companies end up paying higher prices, receiving inferior goods, and losing out on legitimate business opportunities.

Off-books schemes are many times impossible to detect. By "off-books," we mean transactions that don't have anything reflected on the books of the company. If there is no documentation that a transaction occurred to begin with, it's extremely difficult to detect.

However, the continued expansion of electronic transactions has had an interesting effect on fraud. Some may believe that the use of computers and electronic transfers has made fraud easier to commit, but in fact it often creates more of a "paper trail" of activity than a perpetrator may realize. An employee who previously may have received a cash bribe may now receive an electronic transfer of funds. There's no physical check to follow through the banking system, but the electronic transfer has certainly created a trail leading from the person who paid the bribe to the person who received it.

Fraud schemes involving transactions already on the books run a greater risk of discovery. Since we at least know that a transaction exists, the fraud investigator has a starting point for an investigation. That doesn't mean the details of an impropriety will necessarily be found, but the chances of discovery are greater because the investigator has at least a small bit of information about a transaction and its participants.

Bribery and corruption cannot be committed by a single individual. It is a group crime, and that particular aspect of it may increase the chances of its being discovered. It is a simple fact that the more mouths there are to keep quiet, the more chances someone will be given a clue.

The key to detecting bribery and corruption is looking for red flags that might suggest fraud has occurred. It is challenging to look for red flags with the knowledge that much fraud is perpetrated without a paper trail. An investigator may only have limited documentation with which to start, but that is better than nothing, and it's advisable to start there. Investigators should search for the following items:

- **Documentation.** Is the documentation missing or incomplete? Are there discrepancies in dates or other instances of conflicting information? Are there any apparent alterations to the documents?

- **Relationships between bidders and vendors.** Is there an apparent pattern or predictable relationship between the bids of certain vendors? Do any of the vendors have related party issues? Have any of the vendors been known to collaborate (either ethically or unethically) in the past?

- **Related parties.** Is there a related-party situation between company employees and any of the bidding companies or employees? If there is a related party, was that fact revealed in the beginning, or was it concealed?

- **Timing.** Did any of the bidders attempt to speed up or delay the process? Is there an apparent legitimate reason for doing so?

- **Requirements.** Are the company's requirements for the goods or services unusually broad or restrictive? Do the requirements seem geared toward eliminating all but one or two of the potential bidders? Are the requirements unusually vague or open ended?

- **Employees involved.** Is there an unusual involvement in the procurement process, such as a senior-level employee apparently working beneath his or her responsibility level? This unusual involvement could occur either on the side of the company seeking bids or on the part of the vendors.

- **Bids.** Do any of the bids appear to be "dummy" bids by companies unqualified to perform the work? Did some of the bids fail to meet obvious requirements or provisions? Do some of the bids appear hastily and sloppily prepared in order to ensure that another bidder receives the contract?

- **Withdrawal.** Has the lowest bidder withdrawn after the bids have been submitted? Has a bidder been allowed to withdraw from the process without justification or penalty?

- **Selection.** Has a vendor other than the lowest bidder been selected without any apparent legitimate reason? Has a bidder with a poor history of performance been awarded the contract?

Preventing Bribery and Corruption

In order to enter into a corruption scheme, an employee generally must be in a position to participate in a conspiracy with a vendor, and the employee must have some level of authorization within the company. This authorization level varies. It could include the ability to recommend a purchasing contract, authorize vendors, approve payments, manipulate invoices and other documentation, and cover up a fraud.

Yet the answer to preventing bribery and corruption schemes is not in taking away access and authority. The fact remains that companies need employees in positions of trust who can authorize transactions and make judgment calls about the business.

Proper oversight of the purchasing and accounts payable functions is one important step in combating bribery and corruption. Segregation of duties is also helpful. With the two of these in play, it will be much more difficult for a purchasing agent to manipulate contracts, payments, and vendor approval. Simply having additional oversight in this area of the company will deter some people who might have attempted to abuse the system.

Supervision and oversight go beyond routine observance of employees and their work. If a company is trying to prevent bribery and corruption, preventive activities must include regular examination of documentation, both paper and electronic. Management must look for the override of controls, falsified approvals, alteration of documents or approvals, and authenticity of work orders. Purchase orders, receipts, and invoices must be compared against actual products or services received to determine whether the paperwork accurately reflects reality.

Preventing an employee from receiving gifts from an interested party is often difficult, however. It's hard for management to know about these things, much less stop them. One way to deter these activities is to rotate the people who have contact with outside vendors. Frequent rotation of employees prevents them from developing close relationships with any one vendor, and can decrease the likelihood that gifts are being given.

Clear ethics policies can also go a long way toward preventing this type of behavior. It won't stop those who are hell-bent on beating the system or making money any way they can, but it may stop those who are normally honest and will usually abide by the rules. It's important to spell out what is and is not acceptable under the ethics policy, and this may include actually giving some examples of prohibited behavior. For example, not every employee will understand that doing business with a family member could be classed as a conflict of interest, so it might be necessary to illustrate it.

TIPS AND TECHNIQUES

Techniques to Prevent Bribery and Corruption

- Oversight of purchasing and accounts payable
- Segregation of duties
- Examination of documentation
- Job rotation
- Ethics policy

Multinational Issues

Companies doing business in an international marketplace will have numerous experiences involving bribery and corruption. It is important to acknowledge that different cultures have different standards and practices, and certain acts that are considered inappropriate in one country may be perfectly allowable in another county. It is even more important to understand how U.S. laws might affect the practices management may participate in when doing business with foreign companies.

Summary

Asset misappropriation schemes and bribery or corruption schemes are far more common than financial statement fraud, but the individual fraud schemes cost companies less than financial statement fraud. Asset misappropriation fraud involves taking cash and other assets, and various schemes are used to accomplish this. Some of the more common include cash skimming, cash larceny, theft of inventory or equipment, and shell-company scams. This type of fraud is best prevented through segregation of duties, monitoring employees, and examination of accounts and documentation.

Bribery and corruption schemes are aimed at providing an advantage or some other benefit to the recipients. Included in this category of fraud are kickbacks, bid rigging, and conflicts of interest. These schemes are often harder to detect than other frauds because the victim company may have little or no information that even points to the existence of a fraud scheme. Bribery and corruption schemes can be prevented through careful monitoring of relationships between employees and interested parties. Probably the most effective tool in preventing this type of fraud is the establishment of an ethical corporate culture.

Notes

1. 2006 Report to the Nation, Association of Certified Fraud Examiners, Austin, TX.
2. Ibid.
3. Ibid.
4. Ibid.

Financial Statement Fraud

After reading this chapter, you will be able to

- Identify the most common ways financial statements are fraudulently manipulated.
- Recognize some of the common red flags of financial statement fraud.
- Understand why traditional independent audits fail to detect fraud most of the time.

Financial statement fraud is a means to an end. It doesn't result in a direct financial benefit to anyone. Rather, it provides an indirect benefit, in the form of increased stock prices, a greater value to stock options, continued bank financing, a periodic bonus, a promotion, or a host of other financial results.

Avoiding "failure to perform" for the stock market can be a huge incentive for financial statement fraud. What company wants to miss earnings expectations and take a hit to its stock price? Failure to perform is also a fear on the individual level, and executives with jobs and promotions at stake sometimes give in to the temptation to manipulate the financial statements.

The true cost of financial statement fraud is quite likely underestimated by the business world at large. A CPA once theorized out loud that there wasn't really any "cost" to financial statement fraud, as the problem was really only a matter of ink on paper. He said the wrong numbers were printed on the paper, and there wasn't a cost to that. Of course, he was wrong. Very wrong.

Financial statement fraud is the most costly type of fraud committed at companies. Although financial statement fraud is present in only about 10% of internal fraud cases, the median cost of a financial statement fraud is $2 million.[1]

The enormous cost related to this category of fraud is likely a result of some of the characteristics of the perpetrators discussed in Chapter 2. Those in a position to engineer a large financial statement fraud are generally senior-level executives. These executives have the most access to information, systems, and assets, and can more easily use this access to carry out a fraud.

Additionally, because there is typically collusion in a financial statement fraud, the dollar losses are likely to be higher. This type of fraud usually cannot be carried out by a single perpetrator; often it requires the participation of several people in the company to initiate fraudulent transactions, see to it that they are recorded on the books, and ultimately conceal the fraud.

In addition to creating the largest dollar losses, financial statement frauds often have an impact on many more people than other types of frauds. A financial statement fraud can affect shareholders, investment banks, and scores of employees.

Public Company Financial Statements

In addition to preparing financial statements in accordance with Generally Accepted Accounting Principles (GAAP), public companies are required by the Securities and Exchange Commission (SEC) to make disclosures about the company's operations and numbers. While the numbers on the face of the financial statements help users of the statements to assess the quantitative aspects of the company, the additional disclosures help users evaluate some of the qualitative issues.

Companies engaging in fraud might make inadequate disclosures, fail to disclose issues at all (also called nondisclosure), or make false disclosures. These may all be cause for action by the SEC against a company and its officers and directors.

However, it may be difficult to detect fraud in these disclosures. While some defenders of public companies may suggest that companies are generally forthcoming in these disclosures, how do we know that to be true? Without the benefit of being inside a company, a user of the financial statements has nothing against which to gauge the disclosures. That is, an outsider has no way of knowing whether the disclosures are accurate or adequate.

Executives know what users expect from a company's financial statements. If the numbers don't fall within certain parameters, questions will likely be raised. So the clever executive will ensure that the financial statements meet expectations on certain key measures. The fraud in the financial statements will be well hidden in the numbers, and a good investigator must look far beyond the numbers for evidence of fraud.

Fraud Schemes

Financial statement fraud can include the deliberate misstatement of numbers, caused by booking false accounting entries. It can also happen through the deliberate misapplication of accounting rules. Either way, the financial statements are purposely inaccurate.

It's important to know that mistakes are not fraud. Errors are committed all the time in the accounting and financial reporting process. What distinguishes fraud from errors is the intent behind the actions. It is sometimes difficult to determine which is in play when financial statements are misstated.

One of the first defenses often raised is that of a "mistake." The investigator is left to prove intent, which is not necessarily an easy thing to do. Short of an admission from the perpetrator, intent is most often proved through circumstantial evidence. That is, the facts and circumstances surrounding a fraud demonstrate the intent.

Intent can be proved by the existence of concealed or destroyed evidence, as well as altered documentation. It can usually be said that a person who is behaving honestly (and possibly just made a mistake) would have little or no reason to hide, alter, or destroy evidence. False statements or other obstruction of an investigation may also point to the intent of the accused. A pattern of questionable behavior and unacceptable transactions may also point to intent, and certainly the receipt of direct or indirect benefits from a fraud may signal intent as well.

One common phrase associated with financial statements is "earnings management." Some will tell you that this isn't fraud; it comes right up to the line and does not cross over. Others believe that this is clearly fraud. "Earnings management" is really a phrase to be used when we can't bring ourselves to say the word "fraud."

Managing earnings isn't a noble effort. It is the purposeful manipulation of account balances to make the financial statements conform to some predetermined template. Especially with public companies, there are expectations related to the financial results, and executives may alter numbers to conform. It is easy to justify such behavior when the manipulation occurs with accounts that are heavily influenced by the judgment of management, such as reserve accounts. This doesn't make the practice right, however.

IN THE REAL WORLD

Earnings Management

As "Chainsaw" Al Dunlap and his management team attempted to turn around Sunbeam, they manipulated earnings to make the company look more attractive to Wall Street and potential buyers of the company.

The manipulation started with a too-large accrual for restructuring costs at the end of 1996. Although this reserve increased Sunbeam's losses in 1996, it provided a "cookie jar" that could be used in future years to make results look better than they really were. The reserves were reversed during 1997, and the financial statements falsely showed that Sunbeam's revenue was growing significantly.

An investigation later revealed that Sunbeam's 1997 earnings were overstated by at least $60 million on total earnings from continuing operations of $189 million. The overstatement was more than 30% of the reported earnings from operations.

Adding insult to injury, management failed to disclose that part of the revenue growth was due to discounts given to customers who purchased early. This would impact future periods, when normal purchases by those same customers would not occur.

Overstating Revenue

The most common financial statement manipulation relates to sales. It is in the company's best interest to have higher sales, as opposed to lower sales, so the risk of overstating sales is present in virtually every company. In some industries, it's easy to tell when a sale has occurred. Someone has entered a store, selected an item, and given the cashier money. That is a straightforward transaction that does not need any interpretation.

In more complex industries, when a sale has occurred and when it has not may not be so easily defined. Consider an industry such as insurance, in which a customer usually prepays for the service. Although money has changed hands, the insurance company cannot just recognize a sale immediately. GAAP rules require that the company actually have earned the revenue before it may be recorded as a sale.

This can become increasingly complex for companies that enter into very large, long-term contracts with customers who agree to purchase a certain amount of the product or service. Varying contract terms can affect when revenue may be recognized from these transactions.

The more complicated the transaction or the accounting rules, the greater the risk that revenue may be misstated. And I think a pretty compelling argument could be made that companies usually aren't going to err on the side of booking too little revenue. Although "conservatism" is a basic accounting concept, companies don't always follow that guideline. Companies should be conservative with their estimates instead of being too aggressive, and this definitely applies to the recognition of revenue.

Revenue overstatement can also occur in a much more straightforward fashion, and that is through booking revenue for sales that have not occurred. In this case, there is no gray area. It might include booking a completely fictitious sale. It may also include booking a sale on an item for which title has not passed.

Take for example a company that manufactures large equipment. The company has completed a machine, and the machine is sitting in the plant while the customer's financing arrangements are completed. Clearly, title has not passed and the sale is not completed, as the machine still sits in the manufacturer's plant while details are finalized. Booking a sale for this item would be inappropriate.

IN THE REAL WORLD

Revenue Overstatement

Companies like Enron can find themselves in deep trouble when they recognize revenue from a long-term contract immediately upon signing the papers. Recognizing that revenue immediately gave

Understating Expenses

Simply not booking expenses as they are incurred is one surefire way to increase a company's earnings and enhance the financial statements. The manipulation of expenses can be very straightforward. A company can hold expenses and wait to book them until future periods.

Instead of booking an expense, a company could improperly capitalize an item. Take, for example, a car dealership that had large advertising expenses. During a period of depressed sales, the owner of the dealership was worried about presenting the true financial results to the auto maker. Therefore, several months' worth of advertising expenses was capitalized. Not only did the income statement improve immediately, the balance sheet looked better too because current assets were increased.

A company with a large construction project may also utilize the financial statement fraud method rather easily. As buildings and equipment are rapidly being added to the balance sheet, it might go unnoticed if management plugs some expenses into fixed assets. Again, this would create an instant improvement in the company's financial picture, and the risk of detection of the inflated fixed assets is low.

Companies may also manipulate expenses by failing to write down assets such as accounts receivable, inventory, or buildings and equipment to the correct values under the accounting rules. There are many instances in which companies should book an expense and create a reserve for an asset whose value is impaired. It is tempting to ignore this rule.

Finally, companies can reduce their expenses by failing to report sales discounts, returns, and allowances. Failing to account for such items effectively reduces the company's expenses, and additional profit falls right to the bottom line. This is also an area of the financial statements that may not be heavily scrutinized, minimizing the chance of detection.

IN THE REAL WORLD

Underreporting Expenses

From 1992 through 1997, Waste Management, Inc. executives participated in a systematic scheme to falsify the company's financial results. They underreported expenses to the tune of $1.7 billion, which increased net income by the same amount. Quarterly financial statements were adjusted to align Waste Management's results with predetermined earnings targets. By meeting earnings targets, management received performance-based bonuses and valuable stock options.

Overstating Assets

Manipulation of asset accounts is often done to enhance a balance sheet, especially the important ratios involving assets. At particular risk for overstatement are current assets such as accounts receivable. It is not fun to write down or reserve for outstanding balances that customers will never pay. Yet the accounting rules require this to be done if it is determined that an account is uncollectible.

As noted in the previous section, failing to expense items in favor of improperly capitalizing them is a technique commonly used in financial statement fraud. Accounts with a large amount of activity during a given accounting period are ripe for fraud, as additions to those accounts are less likely to be thoroughly scrutinized.

Other techniques include failing to write down assets with impaired values, such as goodwill or other intangible assets. Companies may also resist writing down obsolete inventory or other assets with impaired values or collection problems.

Understating Liabilities

Liabilities are understated in order to make the balance sheet look better. Less money owed to outside parties means a stronger balance sheet and better ratios when comparing debts to assets and equity. One sneaky way to hide liabilities is by booking them as equity instead. Again, this can dramatically improve the balance sheet.

Manipulations may also be aimed at moving liabilities between current and long-term liability accounts. Management may be willing to report the proper liabilities in total but may wish to juggle items between current and long-term, depending on what their loan covenants require and what future financing plans the company may have.

The most straightforward way to understate liabilities is by not recording money owed to others. The company could hold a bill and wait until next quarter to record it, or management could fail to do something like properly accrue wages owed at the end of an accounting period. Companies could also fiddle with reserves, which will be discussed in detail next.

The flip side of not recording proper liabilities is that expenses are likely to be understated, and therefore the income statement is enhanced. These manipulations of the financial statements don't happen in a vacuum. One manipulation may affect many accounts on the face of the financial statements.

Improper Use of Reserves

Commonly abused accounts include reserves for accounts receivables, sales returns, warranties, and inventory obsolescence. These accounts are inherently risky accounts because they require a great deal of judgment when determining the balance at the end of a period. Management is entrusted with applying its best judgment to these accounts to fairly calculate and estimate the proper reserves.

Because the accounts require judgment and estimates, it's not very easy for auditors to challenge the calculated reserves. Management may provide reasonable and believable explanations for why the reserve balances are what they are. Only time will tell whether those numbers were correct.

Reserves that are too low will understate expenses in the current period, inflating earnings. Down the road the company will have to play "catch up" and recognize higher expenses to make up for the inadequate reserves. That will have a negative impact on the earnings of the future period.

Conversely, management may book reserves that are higher than necessary in the current period. This sometimes happens when a company has had an exceptional quarter or year. The company doesn't "need" to show such high earnings, and may inflate a reserve account and corresponding expense. This reserve can then be used as a "cookie jar" in future periods. The company can reverse out the excess part of the reserve in order to increase earnings in a period that may be a bit down.

Reserves are especially vulnerable to abuse because so many users of financial statements do not truly understand how reserves really work. They wouldn't be able to determine whether a reserve is understated or overstated in a period. They may not even be able to explain what a reserve is or does. That lack of understanding is easy to exploit.

IN THE REAL WORLD

Improper Use of Reserves

During 1996, First Merchants Acceptance Corp. experienced rising delinquent accounts receivable. To avoid charging off the uncollectible accounts, the company manipulated the accounts receivable to make more than 7,000 delinquent accounts appear current. As a result, net income was overstated by $76.7 million, for which the Securities and Exchange Commission took action.

Mischaracterization as One-Time Expenses

Another way to manipulate the financial statements is by characterizing normal, recurring expenses as one-time or nonrecurring. This effectively removes them from the heart of the financial statements (operations) and puts them in an entirely separate category.

By removing the expenses from operations, users of the financial statements are given a false impression of the true operating results. What should be classified as normal expenses in operating the business are falsely characterized as something that won't occur in the future.

How would a user of an income statement know whether something is truly a "one-time" expense or not? What about a company that repeatedly books one-time charges? At some point aren't those one-time charges considered to be recurring if they occur quarter after quarter or year after year?

This type of manipulation may be easy to get away with. The restructuring of a business or the divestiture of a division can be expensive. Financial statement users expect to see large numbers. It's not too difficult to puff up those numbers a little bit to hide other problems within the company.

Misapplication of Accounting Rules

Reasonable people can disagree on the correct application of an accounting rule. It is true that there are some gray areas, and it may take significant research and debate in order to determine the correct application of the rules.

When fraud is being committed, these gray areas are exploited. They're not discussed and debated with the goal of determining the correct way to treat a transaction. Rather, the gray areas provide an opportunity to force an accounting treatment that is beneficial to the fraud scheme.

One red flag of fraud is the unusual application of an accounting rule, especially when that unusual application significantly enhances the financial picture of the company. When an executive is especially vehement in promoting this unusual accounting treatment, it casts further suspicion on the situation.

Misrepresentation or Omission of Information

Financial statements of public companies are filed with the SEC with many notes and explanations attached. These notes and explanations are required to be made so that the user of the financial statements can find them meaningful. Without the notes, it may be difficult to understand the company's business and financials.

In general, companies are required to include notes and explanations about items that are material to the financial statements. One way to defraud and mislead the users of financial statements is by omitting information from these notes or providing deliberately misrepresented information.

Consider, for example, a company that may be subject to a proposed federal law that impacts its industry. That company may need to disclose in the financial statements that the law is pending, and what impact it may have on the company if passed. That sounds pretty straightforward, but it is not necessarily so. What if the company first responded to the makers of the proposed law that such a law would have dire and devastating consequences on the business? Then, the company turns around and discloses in the financial statements that the proposed law would only cause a minor change in the business. Is this disclosure in the financial statements consistent with the devastating consequences told to the lawmakers, or is it misleading? It seems as though it is meant to be misleading, and it attempts to keep from the users of the financial statements the real potential impact of the law.

This is just one short example of the way that shareholders, banks, and other users of financial statements can be misled by the disclosures of management. It is easy to see why companies may be reluctant to report negative information, but that does not excuse them from doing so.

One commonly omitted disclosure is that of material liabilities. Companies are generally required to disclose pending lawsuits or other situations that might require the company to pay out a material amount.

Significant events should also be disclosed, and these might include such things as new product or service offerings, key alliances with vendors or customers, obsolescence of inventory, or any other event that could have a material impact on the financial statements.

A change in the application of accounting rules must also be disclosed with the financial statements, and this is sometimes not done. Users of financial statements need to be able to compare financial statements from period to period; without disclosure of a new accounting rule or a change in how an accounting rule is being applied, the users cannot do so.

Materiality

Sometimes the manipulation of financial statements is justified by management because the manipulation is deemed "immaterial." In monetary terms, a material item is one that is large enough to matter to the financial statements as a whole. Yet the issue of what is material can and should go beyond absolute numbers.

In reality, "material" is used to refer to an item that would change the judgment or decision of a user of the financial statements. For a company that does $5 billion in sales each year, changing a number on the financial statements by $10 million or $20 million may not have much of an effect on the face of the financial statements. Therefore, many may consider those amounts too small to matter and immaterial.

But what about the circumstances behind that $10 million or $20 million? What if that was the amount of theft committed by the company's chief financial officer (CFO)? Might it matter that the company's accounting head was engaged in theft? Might it be important that at least one person in the executive ranks was engaged in a fraud? Would it affect the judgment of a user of the financial statements, such as a banker or a stockholder? If the answer to those questions is "yes," then a theft of that "small" size to a larger company might still be material.

It's important to know that the accounting rules and regulations in the United States do not allow for the use of *only* quantitative measures of materiality. Those measures are most often cited and accepted as the bottom line, but accounting pronouncements specifically say that other situational considerations must be examined as well.

Materiality

The president of a university was terminated due to theft of donor funds. A look at his tenure with the school showed impressive statistics. Fundraising during his presidency was at an all-time high, and enrollment and retention of students was up as well. He seemed like the perfect president for the university, until it was discovered that he was engaged in a fraud that went on for several years.

Were there any warning signs? Yes. It was well known among staff members that the president of the university cheated on his expense reports. Even with a comfortable salary and many expensive perks, he still felt compelled to steal an additional $10 on cab rides and other small amounts.

No one thought the small thefts mattered. After all, they were immaterial to the school's financial position, and the president was the best fundraiser the school ever had. Surely the university could "afford" his expense report indiscretions.

Even though the amounts the president stole on his expense reports were not material, the totality of the situation was material. Had the auditors been informed that he was engaging in a known (albeit small) fraud, they might have altered some of their procedures to uncover the much larger fraud of donor funds far earlier.

Why Financial Statement Audits Don't Find Fraud

With the potential for all this financial statement fraud out there, some people rest easy knowing that companies have independent audits. They assume that the independent audits will guard against fraud and will detect fraud if it is occurring. Even board members and executives of companies often believe that outside auditors will find fraud if it exists within the company. Nothing could be further from the truth.

In fact, the Association of Certified Fraud Examiners' 2006 Report to the Nation found that companies with external audits did *not* have lower fraud losses than those without.[2] External audits were responsible for detecting fraud in only 12% of the cases examined for the report.[3]

Users of financial statements (investors, banks, the general public) are often confused about what an audit is and is not. Specifically as it relates to fraud, the users of financial statements are quite often mistaken about the auditor's responsibility to find fraud.

Unfortunately, when fraud is committed the accounting system and its processes are violated. Improper transactions are completed, and actions are taken to conceal the true nature of these transactions. So normal testing of transactions during a financial statement audit can't possibly deal with this effectively. Audit procedures have never been meant to ferret out fraud.

The absolute bottom line is that detecting fraud is not the main objective of a financial statement audit. Audits and reviews are procedures performed on the financial statements of a company for the purpose of determining whether the financial statements include any material misstatements.

Auditors can't possibly examine each and every transaction a company makes throughout the year. They can't even check "most" of the transactions, or even "many" of the transactions. Therefore, the auditors use sampling techniques to test certain transactions during the performance of an audit or review.

The sampling may be aimed at the largest items or the items on the financial statements that pose the greatest risk of misstatement. If material errors in the financial statements are discovered during this sampling, the auditors will direct management to correct them.

If the sampled transactions are accurate and complete, it is generally assumed that the untested transactions must be accurate and complete as well. If fraud didn't exist, that might be a valid assumption. All other things being equal, if the accounting system works and the tested transactions are properly recorded, then it's a fair assumption that the untested transactions are equally as accurate.

The problem is that misstatements (wrong numbers) in the financial statements can be caused by either error or fraud. Errors are much more likely than fraud to be discovered during an independent audit. Fraud schemes are crafted to purposely exploit the accounting system and controls, and therefore it is more difficult for an auditor to discover them. Since auditors are not all-knowing beings, the assurance that the financial statements are correct can only be "reasonable" assurance, not total assurance.

IN THE REAL WORLD

Why Audits Don't Find Fraud

The bookkeeper at a small nonprofit organization was stealing for several years and cleverly covering her tracks. She didn't let individual checks to herself get too large, and she divided the check amounts between many accounts so that the entries in each account would remain small. She knew that if the amounts were small enough, they probably would not be carefully examined during the annual audits.

She was right, and her scheme worked until an auditor found a problem with the bank reconciliation while dong a project not directly related to the annual audit. That problem led to further investigation, which ultimately uncovered the fraud. The fraud was essentially discovered by accident.

The board of the directors wondered why the auditors hadn't found the fraud sooner, since it had been ongoing for at least three years. The answer was simple. The auditors followed the rules, but those rules aren't always effective at uncovering a situation that is purposely disguised by a dishonest employee.

The bookkeeper used what she knew about the accounting process and the year-end audit to escape detection. She knew that management wasn't checking her work or monitoring the bank account. By utilizing small-dollar transactions, recording false transactions in the accounting system, and discarding canceled checks, she successfully beat the system and ran off with hundreds of thousands of dollars.

Auditing Rules

It's important to understand the guidance given to auditors on the topic of fraud. Accountants performing audits in the United States follow Generally Accepted Auditing Standards (GAAS) in their performance of audits. Additional guidance is provided in the Statements on Standards for Auditing and Review Services (SSARS) and Statements on Auditing Standards (SAS). These sets of authoritative guidance outline the responsibilities that auditors have for finding fraud while performing audits and reviews.

SAS No. 99, "Consideration of Fraud in a Financial Statement Audit," became effective in late 2003. It replaced SAS 82, and was intended to improve auditor performance and increase the likelihood that auditors will detect fraud. However, the truth is that the newer standard did not change an auditor's responsibility to detect fraud. That level of responsibility is low.

Even though SAS 99 does require auditors to perform certain procedures, such as brainstorming the ways that fraud could be committed and maintaining professional skepticism, that doesn't mean they have a greater responsibility to detect fraud. Independent audits are not designed to detect fraud, and therefore they are not likely to detect fraud. The responsibility for preventing and detecting fraud rests squarely on the shoulders of management.

One big problem with a standard such as SAS 99 is the expectation gap between auditors and the general public. Users of financial statements see a standard like this and are often lulled into a false sense of security. They figure that if there is a whole standard devoted to fraud and financial statements, the auditors must be devoted to finding any fraud that exists. The guidance for auditors is continuously evolving as the accounting profession acknowledges that fraud is becoming a more significant issue for clients, but in the end, the auditors do not have an absolute responsibility for the detection of fraud.

TIPS AND TECHNIQUES

SAS 99 Auditor Requirements

- Brainstorm the ways fraud could be committed.
- Assess identified risks of fraud.

Audit Alternatives

Executives, attorneys, and board members may be left asking themselves why they pay for audits if the procedures will not detect all the potential problems with the numbers. Audits and reviews have their place in the business world because they help companies identify risky areas of the financial reporting process, and they (hopefully) find material errors and frauds. With that it mind, audits and reviews have some limited usefulness.

Since reviews and audits can only provide limited (but not absolute) assurance on the numbers, they are only one part of a company's financial picture. Management that wants to go a step further will look beyond audits and reviews.

Internal control reviews with a "focus on fraud" can help prevent fraud. They probably won't detect old frauds, but the involvement of an anti-fraud professional during the review of controls can help the company identify areas of the company that are most at risk for fraud.

The next step is the development of procedures specifically designed to prevent fraud. This requires management to take a proactive stance against fraud. Because management cannot fully rely on audits and reviews to detect fraud, the better alternative is to shore up controls so that the opportunities for fraud are decreased.

While traditional financial statement audits usually don't find fraud, actual fraud examinations do. The two types of procedures require many of the same skills, including technical accounting knowledge, an understanding of business procedures, and financial statement expertise.

However, fraud examinations and investigations require an additional set of skills. That skill set includes a certain investigative intuition that has been practiced and honed to detect fraud in businesses. Good fraud examiners often can't tell you exactly how or why they were able to find the fraud, because they just know that intuitively they are able to follow the paper trail toward fraud.

At the end of the day, the responsibility for fraud prevention and detection falls on the company's management. Executives and managers must clearly understand the inherent limitations of audits and reviews and recognize that they cannot and will not detect all frauds. Audits and reviews should not be avoided or discarded, but management is advised to add proactive fraud prevention measures to help the company maintain better control over the potential for fraud.

Summary

Financial statement fraud is the least common occupational fraud, but it is easily the most costly.

Revenue overstatement can occur through the early recognition of revenue, the booking of completely fictitious revenue, or an incorrect application of the accounting rules. Expenses can be understated by failing to book expenses, improperly capitalizing expenses, or not booking returns and other credits.

A company can enhance its balance sheet by overstating assets and understating liabilities. Reserve accounts can play a role in this manipulation, and they are very pliable, given that the ending balances require the judgment of management.

A variety of nondisclosures and inadequate disclosures can play a major part in financial statement fraud, because they affect the qualitative aspects of the statements. The classification of expenses as one-time rather than recurring can have a dramatic impact on the perceived financial condition of a company. Other issues, such as pending legislation and pending lawsuits, may require disclosure, but failure to make an adequate disclosure is a common practice among executives committing fraud.

Traditional independent audits most often do not detect fraud. These audits were never designed to detect fraud, and they're not required to detect it. On occasion, an external audit does find fraud, but users of financial statements should not count on this.

Procedures specifically designed to detect fraud are one alternative to help find fraud. Companies should design internal controls with fraud in mind, and have internal audit staff test the controls to see whether they are working. A fraud examination by an outside, independent party may also be effective in finding fraud because the examination is specifically designed to do so.

TIPS AND TECHNIQUES

Methods of Committing Financial Statement Fraud

- Overstating revenue
- Understating expenses
- Overstating assets
- Understating liabilities
- Improper use of reserves
- Mischaracterization as one-time
- Misapplication of accounting rules
- Misrepresentation or omission of information
- Misuse of materiality concepts

Notes

1. 2006 Report to the Nation, Association of Certified Fraud Examiners, Austin, TX.
2. Ibid.
3. Ibid.

CHAPTER 6

Fraud Detection and Investigation

After reading this chapter, you will be able to

- Identify some common ways that fraud is detected within companies.

- Develop a basic investigative policy and create a general plan for dealing with reports of suspected fraud.

- Assemble a competent fraud investigation team to examine cases of suspected fraud.

- Know the options for discipline and legal action once a fraud investigation is concluded.

My favorite part of my job, by far, is getting in the trenches and investigating cases of suspected fraud. Following a trail of money and tying together people is fun and rewarding. The problem is that a company has to actually detect fraud before it can be investigated. That's not always as easy as it seems.

Remember that companies put controls in place to ensure that transactions have proper approval and the numbers are recorded correctly. Some of those controls are effective, others are not. People who commit fraud deliberately try to circumvent that system and exploit any perceived weaknesses. So while a system of controls may be very effective for catching errors, it is not necessarily as effective at catching fraud.

Even when there are systems of checks and balances in place and employees are charged with the task of overseeing one another's work, fraud can occur. When managers and executives override the established policies and procedures, the risk of fraud rises dramatically. The chances that fraud will be detected are also decreased when managers and executives override the system.

Detecting Fraud

According to the Association of Certified Fraud Examiners (ACFE), the most common way internal fraud is detected is through a tip from someone. That tipster could be an employee, an outside vendor, a customer, or an anonymous person. More than 34% of internal frauds are detected with tips,[1] so it's easy to see how important it is for a company to have a way for people to report suspicious activities.

122

It is disturbing, however, to note that 25% of all employee fraud schemes are detected by accident.[2] An accidental detection might include a customer's complaint about an account balance followed by an investigation into that balance that reveals manipulation of the customer's account. Maybe an employee who always opens the mail has an unexpected absence, and someone else collects the mail and finds a notice for unpaid payroll taxes. Another possibility is a phone call that's routed to the wrong person, and the one answering the call inadvertently receives information about a fraud.

Further down the list of ways to detect fraud are internal controls, internal audits, and external audits. It's important to know that audit-related activities aren't nearly as effective at detecting fraud as many may believe. Audits are still an important part of the process, because they do play a role in preventing some fraud from occurring. Yet they should not be heavily relied on to detect fraud.

Detecting fraud committed by senior management is more difficult than detecting the fraud committed by lower-level employees. As we've already learned, senior management has access to much more information and can exercise authority over employees to help conceal a fraud. The ability of executives to override internal controls in order to commit fraud can be wide-reaching.

One logical way to actively look for fraud within a company is through the computer systems. Sophisticated software can track and log computer activity, and companies would be wise to track computer login attempts, password attempts, data access attempts, and the geographic location of computer access attempts. Unusual activity in any of these areas can signal a fraud problem, and tracking these things is simple once the software is in place.

IN THE REAL WORLD

Methods of Detecting Internal Fraud

According to the Association of Certified Fraud Examiners, a tip from a vendor, customer, employee, or anonymous individual is the most common way that occupational fraud is detected. Over 34% of frauds were discovered following a tip.[a]

[a]2006 Report to the Nation, Association of Certified Fraud Examiners, Austin, TX.

Software is also available to analyze data in the accounting system. The software can scan information in the database and identify such red flags as

- **Similar vendor names.** Has an employee been cutting checks to Abbot Consulting, knowing that no one will notice it is not the real vendor, Abbott Consulting? (Notice the two Ts in the real vendor's name, as opposed to one in the impostor's.) This is one way to issue a check that will not raise suspicions, and the fraudster can easily take the check for her or his own purposes.

- **Similar addresses for vendors.** This is one way to identify fake vendors, particularly if the address is the same for many different vendors and the address is a post office box or mail service.

- **Vendor with the same address as an employee.** Has an employee set up a false vendor and sent the checks to her or his residence?

- **New vendors showing a high level of activity.** Is it reasonable to believe that a new vendor would have significant activity immediately, or does our company routinely "try out" new vendors before offering them larger contracts?

- **Established vendors showing a new, higher level of activity.** And no apparent explanation, such as a special project.

- **Payments to unapproved vendors.** Were payments made to companies not approved to do business with our company?

- **Payments or refunds being sent to addresses that differ from the addresses on file in the vendor master file.** Checks should be sent to the "official" address on file, and a payment sent to any other address should be investigated.

- **Recurring similar payment amounts.** Did an employee have a duplicate check issued, believing it would not be detected because both checks matched an invoice amount?

- **Checks issued out of sequence.** Are there missing checks that could be used fraudulently?

- **Manually prepared checks.** At a company with a full computerized accounting system, manually prepared checks should be rare. Normal checks should be processed through the purchasing and accounts payable system, and any checks created manually should be examined.

- **Voids or refunds made by an employee.** Does one employee have an unusually high number of write-offs entered into the system compared with other employees?

- **Voids or refunds made by customer.** Does one customer have a higher than normal amount of write-offs.

Tools to monitor accounting systems do not necessarily have to be highly sophisticated or expensive. If a company hasn't monitored the data before, the first and most important step is to start monitoring something. The company can always increase the sophistication of the monitoring activities as management becomes more familiar with the software and the techniques.

Audits versus Investigations

As we learned in Chapter 5, "Financial Statement Fraud," traditional external audits are not terribly effective in detecting fraud. They can have a slight deterrent effect, and that may be one small part of a company's fraud prevention efforts. But actually finding fraud through independent audits is highly unlikely.

That's where a different type of accountant and a different type of audit come into play. Forensic accountants or fraud examiners conduct investigations, examinations, fraud audits, or procedures that can be referred to by any of a number of other similar terms. Whatever it is called, the examination is specifically geared at gathering evidence of fraud (if any).

The procedures employed by a forensic accountant or fraud examiner may be similar in some ways to the techniques used by traditional auditors. Certainly both jobs require a technical understanding of a business, the financial statements, and the accounting data. However, there is an intangible part of fraud examination that is also vital. It is something that I call a "nose for fraud." It is that intuition and that creativity that allows the investigator to think like a criminal and follow strong instincts to ultimately detect and solve a crime. This investigative intuition must be there for an examination of the technical books and records to be effective.

Another significant difference between a traditional audit and a fraud investigation is the concept of materiality. During a traditional audit, there is generally a dollar figure under which auditors essentially disregard errors or discrepancies. There is no such materiality threshold in a fraud investigation. Any fraud, no matter the size, might be material and should be examined. This is particularly true given the fact that almost all large frauds started as small ones.

Investigative Policy

It is important to implement a standard set of guidelines for managers to follow when fraud is suspected. Most supervisors and managers have never dealt with on-the-job fraud, so they need guidance about the process of evaluating fraud allegations. Further, guidelines may help guard against employees' claims of selective treatment. Most importantly, an investigative policy brings integrity and quality control to the process.

An investigative policy helps management evaluate allegations of fraud and decide when an actual investigation is warranted. The policy may also help to determine how wide-reaching the investigation should be. Additionally, the policy brings uniformity to the process and helps management to treat accusations and offenses similarly.

The first step in creating the policy is developing a series of red flags that will cause management to consider investigating. For example, a credible tip from an employee could be one red flag. Another possibility is an account that can't be reconciled and has unusual accounting entries. These are not detailed red flags; rather, they are broad guidelines that suggest the minimum factors that trigger an inquiry. Those factors, as well as anything more serious, should be immediate cause for further scrutiny.

Decide who is in charge of assessing the red flags and determining the need for an investigation. In many cases, a departmental supervisor can be the appropriate person to evaluate the red flags. The higher the level of the accused, the higher the level of the person in charge of evaluating the situation should be. For example, if the chief financial officer (CFO) is potentially involved in a fraud, then the chief executive officer (CEO) or the chairman of the board might be the person to examine the situation and determine whether an investigation is warranted.

It may also be appropriate to have more than one level of management involved in the process. Some corporations are more comfortable with multiple levels of scrutiny prior to initiating a full-blown investigation. For example, an area manager may gather information about a potential fraud and present it to a higher-level manager; working together, they decide how to proceed.

The investigative policy should then dictate the triggers for taking action. What criteria should be met for a high-level examination to begin? What must happen for management to decide to skip the high-level examination and move straight into a full-blown investigation? If a high-level examination is made, what criteria will then call for escalating the process to a full investigation?

There may not be a black and white answer for every situation in reaching a decision to make only a quick review or to proceed with a thorough investigation. Many situations, however, will probably have a clear line of demarcation. For example, unusual accounting entries in an unimportant account may require only a small amount of research to resolve. However, a check with a forged endorsement may be cause for an all-out investigation.

After an analysis has been completed, a decision must be made about future action. One option is to forgo monitoring, because the situation at hand was determined to be an innocent mistake or had some other reasonable explanation. Another situation might not yield any concrete results when reviewed but still might cause management to monitor an employee or department on an ongoing basis.

The most serious situations will require disciplinary action against one or more employees. Naturally, depending on the seriousness of the infraction, that discipline might range from a verbal reprimand all the way to dismissal and legal action. It is helpful to have some guidelines in place regarding the action that will be taken. Those guidelines will differ greatly among companies and industries.

Companies with good internal controls and effective ethics policies should not discount the need for fraud investigations. Even the most ethical corporate cultures experience fraud, and investigations are necessary to discover the details of the frauds. Further, investigations send a message to employees that fraud will be fully investigated and resolved. This can have a deterrent effect on employees who may be considering engaging in unethical behavior.

People will always "test the system" as well as look for ways to beat the system and get around internal controls. Investigations must occur to let these scofflaws know that the company is actively pursuing dishonest activities.

Investigative Policy Checklist

- Which red flags cause a company to consider an investigation?
- Who is in charge?
- What triggers a high-level examination?
- When should a company escalate to a full-blown investigation?
- What results cause a company to monitor employees?
- What results trigger disciplinary action?

Investigative Team

The first step in a full-blown fraud investigation is creating a team of qualified professionals. Some team members may be employees of the company, while others might more appropriately be outside consultants. Auditors, both internal and external, can play an important role in a fraud investigation, but they should not have primary responsibility for the investigation. Rather, a fraud examiner or forensic accountant with experience investigating and analyzing fraud should be "in charge" of the investigation. The auditors will support the investigation with information on company procedures and controls, but they typically don't have the same skill sets and experience as fraud examiners.

An additional benefit of bringing in a fraud examiner or forensic accountant is the independence that person brings to the project. An internal or external auditor may have a level of familiarity with personnel and the operations that may cause her or him to not be completely independent. In addition, a fresh set of eyes looking at the company may be able to discover something new related to the investigation.

Legal counsel should be a strong part of the team, often dictating the direction of the investigation. While the fraud examiner or forensic accountant will be the one to plan and perform the investigation, the attorney will have an end result in mind and can point the investigation in the right direction. For example, a case that will probably be litigated might require a somewhat different investigation than one that is being pursued primarily for the purpose of shoring up internal controls in the future. For this reason, I like to have the attorney head up the investigation. The best investigations are often those in which the attorney determines the overall objective of the investigation, but the fraud investigator guides the activities to secure the right evidence for the case.

A management representative and a representative of the board of directors should be involved in the investigation as well. They definitely need to know about the potential fraud, and ought to have a say in the investigation. While the fraud examiner or forensic accountant can probably provide the best guidance about the direction of the investigation, management and the board may also have valuable input.

The management representative should be someone superior to the person or persons being investigated. Thus, if an accounting clerk is suspected of theft, it might be best to have her or his direct supervisor fill this role. If the CFO is suspected of fraud, the likely management candidate for the investigation team is the CEO. However, if there are uncertainties as to the involvement of other senior-level managers in a fraud scheme, they most definitely should not be involved in the investigation. In this case, one or two representatives of the board of directors or owners' group should be the ones who join the investigative team.

Other company representatives who may play a minor role in a fraud investigation include people from human resources and corporate security. Human resources people are important because they possess personnel records, which may be needed for the investigation or legal proceedings. Their input may also be helpful if an employee is to be disciplined or terminated. Corporate security can bring skill sets to the table that go beyond physical security records. They are often former law enforcement officers who can lend investigative expertise, interviewing skills, or other qualities useful to the company.

Companies should consider using outside consultants when necessary in an investigation—for example, a computer forensics expert. Oftentimes, companies discipline employees and secure their company-owned personal computers. They then have the information technology (IT) department look at the computer for evidence of misdeeds. Unfortunately, those who are inexperienced in the rules of evidence may actually destroy evidence in an attempt to find it. Therefore, a better option is to bring in a consultant who secures digital evidence for a living.

If law enforcement agents have been notified of a crime, the investigators should work carefully with them. While cooperation is important, law enforcement should not be considered part of the company's "team." The investigators can gather information that will be helpful to the police, but their work should not be solely dictated by law enforcement.

Police do not work for the company, and the investigators do not work for the police. However, if we can provide information and documentation that helps the criminal case, we certainly want to do that. And if there are specific things they do not want us to do, such as interviewing suspects, it is important to honor that in order to preserve the criminal case.

TIPS AND TECHNIQUES

Investigative Team

- Fraud examiner or forensic accountant
- Internal and external auditors
- Legal counsel
- Management representative
- Board of directors representative
- Human resources
- Corporate security
- Outside consultants

Managing the Process

As with any project, there must always be one captain of the ship. Notice I say "one," because it is too confusing to have more than one person in charge. On my investigations, the lead attorney is in charge of the investigation. This means that the attorney gives direction to the process and makes major decisions based on the litigation that is planned.

The fraud examiner or forensic accountant should lead the actual investigative field work. Anyone assisting with the actual investigation should report to this person, so that there is a central point at which to gather all data.

Good document management procedures are critical, especially in an investigation that is document intensive. It's important to organize the documents properly from the start, so that the team doesn't have to go back through boxes and boxes of papers when it decides that the initial process was inadequate. I recommend organizing documents chronologically, and possibly also separating documents by witness or transaction. For example, a fraud involving an employee and three outside vendors may be best organized by vendor, and then within each of those three vendor boxes, sort documents by date.

A database or spreadsheet for tracking documents is also helpful, and the sophistication of that will probably depend on how large and complex the case is. When tracking documents, my purpose is twofold. First, I want to be able to quickly locate a document if I need it. Second, if someone asks if I saw document XYZ, I want to be able to quickly determine whether or not I have it in my possession.

When logging documents into a database or spreadsheet, I like to track the date of the document (if there is one), the source from which I received it, the date on which it was received, a very brief description of it, and who or what may be associated with it. For example, if there are three suspects in an embezzlement scheme and there is a paper showing a false journal entry generated by suspect C, I will log the details of the document and note that it is related to suspect C.

It's often helpful to keep a "key document file" in addition to all the boxes of documents you may have. Certain key pieces of evidence are copied, and the copy is kept in a separate file for quick access. For example, a closing statement for an important real estate transaction or an account statement for a vendor of interest may need to be referenced quickly and often. The original documents will stay in the proper box or file, but a copy will be made to be kept in the key document file for easy referencing.

One of the most important parts of managing the investigative process is properly supervising staff, particularly if the staff is generally inexperienced with investigating fraud. The person supervising the staff ought to be an experienced investigator. That supervisor should make sure that proper investigative techniques are used, evidence is preserved, and the work is thorough.

Finally, it's important to maintain the integrity of the investigation. Part of this includes maintaining confidentiality throughout the process. Only those who really "need to know" should be informed that a fraud investigation is in process. An internal fraud often damages the morale of employees, and there is no need to constantly remind them of the fraud by making a big deal of the investigation. In fact, if investigators are able to effectively complete their work off site, that may be the best way to go.

TIPS AND TECHNIQUES

The Scope of an Investigation Is Influenced By:

- **Potential dollar losses.** Larger losses likely mean a larger investigation is in order.

- **Odds of recovery and amount of expected recovery.** The less likely we are to recover stolen funds, the less we probably want to spend on the investigation.

- **Insurance coverage.** If an insurance policy may cover the loss, the policy language may influence the investigation to some degree.

- **Size of budget.** What the company can "afford" will play a part in determining how wide-reaching the investigation will be.

- **Ability to perform tasks internally versus using outside consultants.** If company personnel can competently perform some tasks without compromising the integrity of the investigation, that may allow the company to undertake a wider investigation.

- **Goals of owners and executives.** Management may decide on a detailed investigation, in spite of other factors that might suggest that a smaller scope is sufficient.

- **Legal action.** A potential civil or criminal action against the perpetrator may serve to widen the scope of an investigation.

The Investigation

A description and discussion of a full-blown fraud investigation can fill a book in and of itself. Naturally, the exact procedures followed will vary with the type of case. Some of the general highlights of fraud investigations do merit mentioning, however.

The purpose of a fraud investigation is to gather evidence of a fraud, if any. Although allegations of fraud may have prompted the investigation, the investigator must be objective in her or his work, attempting to determine whether or not a fraud has actually been committed.

Evidence of embezzlement or other fraud does not just include documentation such as paper, computer files, or other written or printed sources. It also includes testimony received from interviews and interrogations, physical evidence such as fingerprints and stolen objects, personal observation on the part of the fraud investigators, and information collected through surveillance and covert operations.

One of the key aspects of conducting an effective investigation is knowing when to outsource certain parts of it. For example, most in-house IT departments are not skilled at performing computer forensic work. Gathering evidence from computers and properly preserving it for court activity is an art unto itself, and shouldn't be left to IT people who lack this specialized training. An outside specialist should be brought in to gather digital evidence, to restore evidence that may have been deleted or altered, and to testify in the future about the evidence.

Performing analytical procedures at the beginning of an investigation can yield some interesting results. Sometimes a company is aware that a fraud has occurred, but has no idea where in the accounting system the theft is buried. Horizontal ratio analysis can point to differences in account balances from one year to the next. Sometimes the percentage change from year to year is unusual, and other times the difference in dollars between the years is what's important. Vertical ratio analysis can highlight items that are unusual as a percentage of sales. Although ratio analysis is only a tiny part of a fraud investigation, it can be a tool that leads the investigator to question certain financial items.

The heart of a fraud investigation is examination of documents, including both paper documents and digital evidence. I like to think of this document examination as an audit on steroids. Consider the documents examined by auditors during a financial statement and multiply those by 10, or 100, or 1,000, or even more. A fraud investigation involves intensive scrutiny of details, and the number of documents examined often dwarfs the number of those examined during a traditional audit.

Fraud investigators are notorious for looking at many, many details. This may include examination of bank statements, canceled checks, vendor invoices, accounting system reports, purchasing and inventory records, payroll records, internal and external emails, along with various other documents. Of course, the amount and type of documentation examined depends on the scope of the investigation.

In addition to making a detailed examination of the company's books and records, fraud investigators may also wish to see other indirectly relevant documentation. This may include prior audit and investigation files, which can give insight into the operations of the company along with prior fraud matters. Personnel records for alleged perpetrators can give background information that may be helpful for further investigation. The fraud examiner may wish to examine corporate policies and procedures, as well as official company communications to employees.

Security logs and records may be requested by a fraud investigator as well. She or he may wish to examine logs regarding access to buildings or secured areas, and video evidence can be helpful. Finally, computer access records, detailing which username accessed which records at what time, can be another important source of information.

There are plenty of public records that are available to assist in investigating people, companies, and transactions. The challenge is finding the right source for the records. The sources range from free to paid, and it's important to work with someone who knows the most reliable and reasonably priced resources. Many jurisdictions now maintain online court records, which can be a source of information about the people and businesses involved in a potential fraud. Most states provide business registration records online too, and some even provide names of officers and directors of registered corporations. Each day, more and more records are becoming readily available online, and they are an invaluable source of information when trying to connect the dots between people, businesses, and transactions.

Non-public records can easily become a part of a fraud investigation as well. These can include bank and tax records, stock brokerage records, credit reports, credit card statements, telephone records, and more. These records aren't available to the general public and must be requested—sometimes informally, other times formally through a court of law. Don't expect it to be easy to obtain these personal and private records, but sometimes people involved in investigations are motivated to cooperate and voluntarily turn over documents.

Closing the Investigation

A fraud investigation is most often concluded with a written report that details the findings of the fraud examiner and the rest of the team. A good report outlines the case, the documents, and the evidence of fraud in a concise and clear manner. Any technical or accounting language should be clearly defined, and a report should be written so that just about anyone could understand it. The report could end up in front of a jury someday, and the jurors need to be able to use the information it contains.

When an Investigation Reveals Nothing Incriminating

It can be disappointing to investigate a suspected fraud and come to the conclusion that no fraud can be proved. Sometimes this may be because a fraud did not occur, and other times it may be because a fraud was committed but the evidence to prove it has not been found.

What can management do after an investigation fails to yield any results? The best two things a company can do are (1) improve policies and procedures in light of any weaknesses found during the investigation and (2) move on, focusing on growing the business and preventing future frauds.

The report should outline what happened, what documents and evidence were examined, and who was interviewed. It should detail any calculations related to the evidence, and should lay out the findings in a logical format. Complex calculations and voluminous data are probably best left out of the body of the report; instead, they should be attached at the end. A summary of those calculations and data should be in the report.

At this point companies are faced with the decision whether to take legal action or not. Sometimes legal action will already have been initiated by the time an investigation closes, but many times the "powers that be" are waiting for the results of the investigation before they decide on legal action.

Ideally, management would present the fraud examiner's findings to the thief and the thief would confess to all the misdeeds and then return all the money. Unfortunately, this almost never happens. On occasion, a defrauded company receives a settlement from a fraudster, but this is not as common as many would hope.

Civil actions are possible, but sometimes the cost of pursuing the fraudster is higher than any potential recovery. I like to point out that most thieves are not stealing to save. They are stealing to spend. Many times the idea of recovering the proceeds of fraud is merely a fantasy. What about the assets of the thief? Often there are few collectible assets, but it doesn't hurt to look into whether or not the thief has some home equity or other assets to seize.

A final option is a criminal action, although it can be difficult to get a prosecution. The reality is simple: violent crimes receive most of the criminal justice system's attention. Financial crimes have a much lower priority for most law enforcement agencies. But it can't hurt to inquire with local, state, or federal authorities. Sometimes a law enforcement agency will agree to investigate a case, but other times the agency may be willing to pursue the case only if the company does the bulk of the investigating and bears that cost.

At any rate, prosecutors at various levels are looking for a reason to pursue a case. They know there are plenty of white-collar crimes being committed, and there are limited resources to go after them. Prosecutors may look for a case that seems easy to win. There may also be an incentive to pursue cases that involve prominent people or companies. Frauds involving large sums of money or very egregious acts may also attract the attention of law enforcement.

Whether a matter is brought before a court or not, it is still important for management to use the information obtained in the investigation to improve the company's position. If a discipline policy is not already in place, one should be created with the help of labor and employment attorneys. Discipline is important because it sends a message to would-be fraudsters, so it's important to have a consistently enforced policy.

TIPS AND TECHNIQUES

Disciplinary Options Following the Detection of Internal Fraud

- Verbal or written reprimand
- Punishment such as unpaid suspension or loss of privileges or benefits
- Implementation of a probationary period, during which the employee will be carefully monitored
- Denial of a pending or planned promotion
- Demotion from the current position of authority
- Dismissal from the company
- Civil action to recover proceeds of fraud
- Report of fraud to law enforcement for possible criminal action

Note that any disciplinary action should be fully documented in the employee's personnel records.

Summary

Detecting fraud in companies is difficult, but policies and procedures can be put in place to encourage the reporting of fraud. Tips from employees and customers are some of the most common ways that companies discover in internal fraud, so it makes sense to make it easy for people to report tips. Analysis of a company's documents and databases can also yield information about potential frauds in progress. It's important to periodically examine records to look for evidence of misdeeds. This is especially important because when employees know management is looking for fraud, they are less likely to engage in questionable behavior.

The process of investigating fraud should begin with an investigative policy that guides the actions of management when fraud is suspected. An investigative policy helps bring a level of fairness and consistency to the process and offers some quality control. If an analysis of a situation results in a full-blown investigation, management must assemble a team of qualified, competent professionals to carry out the investigation. This often includes outside, independent parties with expertise in fraud examinations.

The actual investigation may be a lengthy and expensive process. It is important, however, that the investigation be thorough and accurate. Documents and records must be properly secured and indexed so that they may later be used as evidence, if necessary. An examination of the evidence will also likely include examination of computer records, interviews with witnesses and participants, and detailed scrutiny of documentation.

A fraud investigation will likely conclude with a written report of the methods and findings, and management will be left to decide on a course of action. This may include discipline of employees, a civil action against the perpetrator, or a referral to law enforcement. Police agencies are sometimes reluctant to pursue white-collar crimes, but a case that has been fully investigated and presented in an organized and understandable manner has a greater chance of being accepted by law enforcement.

IN THE REAL WORLD

When Privileges Turn into Fraud

When does an abuse of privileges at a company turn into fraud? When does taking advantage of the system cross the line from condoned theft to outright fraud?

This can be a very fine line. I have seen many companies exploited for personal gain, especially those with family members in the executive ranks. The rules may be lax for those executives, and it's often not clear when the executive has crossed over to fraud and abuse.

In one company, the owner's son was allowed liberal use of the company's credit card and fixed assets. He regularly purchased meals and fuel on the company's credit card, even when those expenses were clearly of a personal nature. The owner did not say no until his son crossed the line and issued unauthorized checks to himself. Imagine the son's shock when his father fired him for this transgression.

The lesson from this company can be summed up as follows: Make expectations clear and define acceptable and unacceptable conduct. Apply the company's rules on a consistent basis to all employees.

Notes

1. 2006 Report to the Nation, Association of Certified Fraud Examiners, Austin, TX.
2. Ibid.

CHAPTER 7

Fraud Prevention

After reading this chapter, you will be able to

- Identify the types of internal controls and their importance to the business as a whole.
- Evaluate the control activities within a company and determine the deficiencies from a fraud prevention perspective.
- Discuss the key components of an effective comprehensive fraud prevention program.

The impact of fraud hits a company straight in the bottom line. While large corporations may be able to withstand a six- or seven-figure fraud, a smaller corporation or a nonprofit organization may never recover. To survive in today's competitive marketplace, businesses must be proactive in the fight against fraud.

When accountants think of fraud prevention, they think of internal controls. The outsider asks "What are internal controls?" Internal controls are exactly what they sound like—the set of rules or procedures that control the way things are done within a company. In theory, if the procedures are set up properly and everyone follows them, errors are averted and fraud does not occur.

The problem is that people who commit fraud are intentionally going around, over, and through those internal controls to accomplish their own agendas. They break the rules when they commit the fraud, and then usually break more rules to cover up the fraud.

So why bother with internal controls if fraud still happens? That's easy. Internal controls, when set up correctly, can and do prevent many frauds. People are generally honest, and for them the idea of breaking the rules or circumventing prescribed procedures is unthinkable. And when dishonest employees do commit fraud, good internal controls can help honest employees discover the fraud.

Internal Control Basics

At all times, the management of a company bears ultimate responsibility for establishing, maintaining, and enforcing a secure and controlled system of checks and balances. The cost to create, implement, and maintain effective controls can be high. As with any business decision, it's important to weigh the cost against the benefits that may be achieved with the controls.

Remember, however, that the risk of internal fraud is high. Fraud examiners estimate that 5 to 6% of a given company's revenues are lost to fraud each year. An executive might say, "Not at my company."

It may be true that a particular company hasn't discovered fraud of that magnitude from within. That doesn't mean it's not happening, though. The cost of fraud prevention and management should be weighed against the company's total annual fraud risk before decisions are made about the money to be spent on prevention efforts.

Even when budgetary constraints rule, it is important for management to institute at least some level of controls. There are some checks and balances that are not costly to implement (such as segregation of basic duties, on-time reconciliation requirements, and the like), and those should be done, at a very minimum.

Certainly, some controls can be much more effective and secure than others, but they could also be cost prohibitive. When cost is the overriding consideration, controls should not be ignored altogether, but management should search for the cost-effective method that brings an adequate level of regulation to a risk area.

Internal controls related to fraud fall into one of three categories:

1. **Preventive controls.** These are focused on protecting the company's assets and information by stopping fraud from occurring.

2. **Detective controls.** These are aimed at finding fraud when it occurs, hopefully as soon as possible.

3. **Corrective controls.** These attempt to remedy problems that are discovered, so that future frauds can be better prevented and detected.

All three of these categories are important to an effective set of internal controls. If any one is missing, the other two automatically become less effective. Take for example, corrective internal controls. These might include the prescribed punishment to be imposed after a fraud has been discovered. If a company elects not to punish those who commit fraud, the other processes become immediately less effective because employees observe that policies aren't being enforced. Thus, the policies hold little meaning for employees and they are more likely to violate them.

Internal Controls and Sarbanes-Oxley

The Sarbanes-Oxley Act of 2002 (SOX) generally applies to U.S. public companies and their auditors, but numerous multinational public companies and private companies are complying with the regulations voluntarily. SOX generally requires

- Management to assess the effectiveness of the company's internal control structure over financial reporting. Are the controls effective at ensuring that the financial statements will be presented accurately?

- An auditor's report on management's assessment. Do the auditors believe that management's assessment of the internal controls is accurate?

- New auditing standards and rules for auditing firms with public clients. Auditors of public companies are limited in the other services that they may provide to their clients, in order to ensure their independence.

Other broad requirements of SOX include whistleblower provisions, under which companies must establish a confidential, anonymous reporting mechanism for employees. This is most often accomplished with an anonymous hotline; this can be set up through a vendor, which guarantees anonymity for callers. The company must also disclose whether a Code of Ethics has been established for executives and make it available to the public. SOX defines conflicts of interest and prohibits certain actions, such as personal loans to executive officers or directors.

SOX does not specify a particular set of internal controls that must be in place in companies. There are certain elements of internal controls that are required, such as the whistleblower provisions and management's evaluation of the internal controls, but the regulation does not specify a large set of controls that must be put into place.

Understanding what SOX does *not* require of companies may be even more important than knowing what *is* required. Many individuals and investors do not understand that SOX actually requires very little in the way of substantive improvement to the internal controls of a company. As long as management is willing to admit publicly that its controls are not good, the company is not forced to improve the internal controls.

TIPS AND TECHNIQUES

Considering a Whistleblower Program?

- Anonymous hotlines cut fraud losses in half.
- Tips are the leading method of detecting fraud.

TIPS AND TECHNIQUES (CONTINUED)

- Promote a culture in which employees view whistleblowing as a necessary component of an ethical environment that protects their futures.
- Consider extending the whistleblower program to suppliers, customers, and others outside the organization.
- Programs must be confidential, and whistleblowers must be assured that there will be no retaliation.
- Complaints against senior management must go directly to the audit committee.

Auditing and Internal Controls

As the audits done by independent auditors have become more focused on risk-based procedures, the effectiveness of a company's internal controls has been put in the spotlight.

Risk-based audits focus on identifying the functions and accounts in a company that pose the highest risk for errors or irregularities— that is, the areas that are most at risk for misstatements in the financial statements.

Instead of just looking for the result (misstated financial statements), the auditor is looking for the cause (deficient controls). So the focus is on evaluating quality within the financial reporting process, rather than just examining the accounting records.

Statement on Auditing Standards (SAS) 99, "Consideration of Fraud in a Financial Statement Audit," gives auditors specific guidance on the issue of fraud within a company. This standard requires auditors to identify a company's risk of fraud; they are expected to assume that improper revenue recognition constitutes a fraud risk, as does management override of internal controls.

So auditors may be somewhat more mindful of issues surrounding internal controls and their impact on the financial report. However, this doesn't mean that external auditors are any more likely to detect fraud than they have been in the past.

Control Activities within a Company

The policies and procedures of a company fall into a number of categories, the most common of which are discussed in this section. One of the most obvious parts of a company's set of internal controls is *safeguards over assets*. This means that the company is securing the physical assets through locked doors, secured desks and filing cabinets, locked storage areas, and the use of identification badges. Accurate records of the assets and information owned by the company must also be kept.

Additionally, blank checks are secured, computers are secured with passwords, and data is protected with security software. Access to data is given only to those who need it, and attempts to access the computer system from the outside are controlled and monitored. Limiting access to digital information is especially critical in this information age. Computerized data is vulnerable to hackers and disgruntled employees, and customer information must be guarded diligently.

Segregation of duties is another aspect of internal controls. In smaller companies, it is one of the most widely disregarded internal controls. This is disheartening, as it is not terribly difficult to divide duties between employees so that one employee doesn't have too much control over a given area. Yet smaller companies are reluctant to take this step, because it isn't always easy or efficient to divide tasks among employees. But it only takes one fraud for companies to realize the importance of segregation of duties and the relatively small amount of effort and cost involved compared with the risk of fraud.

The heart of segregation of duties is separating the custodial, recording, and authorization functions throughout the company. For example, in relation to accounts receivable, the custodian would have possession of the assets—the customers' payments in cash or check. The recording function is twofold, including the updating of customer accounts to account for the payments and the recording of the bank deposit. The employee in the authorization function would only be permitted to record adjustments to accounts or authorize other unusual transactions.

By separating all three of these duties, it is less likely that customer payments will be stolen. If the person holding the money steals, this will surface when the customer accounts and the bank account are reconciled by another employee. It's easy to see why the person in possession of the money shouldn't be making entries to customer accounts or bank accounts, or reconciling either of them. It's also clear that at least a third person must be involved in the process to allow for adjustment to accounts, and this shouldn't be the person who had custody of the money, preventing her or him from adjusting accounts to cover a theft.

IN THE REAL WORLD

Segregation of Duties

A small manufacturing company had one person in control of all of the company's accounting processes. The accounting manager retrieved the mail, deposited customer payments, updated customer accounts, recorded the bank account balance, and reconciled the bank statements. He also had the authority to book adjusting entries to the accounting system.

Three years later, it was determined that the accounting manager had stolen a significant sum of money. He stole so much that the company teetered on the edge of bankruptcy.

The theft was made easy because there was no supervision of the accounting function and absolutely no segregation of duties. Without even one other person involved in the customer payment process, it was easy for the accounting manager to take customer payments and adjust customer accounts accordingly to cover the theft. The bank account always balanced because he made adjustments to that account as well.

Proper authorization of transactions relates to the level of authority of employees initiating, approving, and recording transactions. Activities in this category can include sign-off on transactions (either a signature on a paper or a digital approval), verifying that proper authorization had been granted before a transaction was completed, and taking corrective action if transactions are completed without proper authorization.

For example, a company may have a policy that any transaction under $10,000 can be approved by an area supervisor but over that amount the area supervisor's manager must do the approval. This is an example of an authorization control, and further components would include follow-up by someone within the company to verify that the proper level of authorization was being obtained for transactions over $10,000.

It is also important to determine that authorizations are not being falsified. This could happen through a forged signature on a paper, or through unauthorized access to computer data to give an electronic authorization. One final component of checking authorizations is determining whether or not the authorization system is being circumvented. For example, if a $14,000 transaction requires a higher level of authorization, an employee may be inclined to break this down into two $7,000 transactions, thereby negating the need for additional authorization.

One way to examine whether transactions are being processed properly is through *independent checks on performance.* Such checks may include such things as surprise audits of accounts, reconciliation of records, cash drawer counts, and physical inventory counts. For these types of checks to have a degree of independence, they must be performed by someone other than those charged with maintaining the accounts, records, or assets. For example, test counts of inventory should not be made by the employee who oversees the warehouse or the employee who maintains the inventory records. Rather, they should be done by someone outside of those functions, who would have no apparent interest in manipulating any of the counts. That person could be an internal auditor or an accounting clerk who deals only with accounts receivable, and not the inventory records.

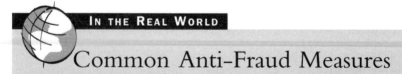

IN THE REAL WORLD

Common Anti-Fraud Measures

According to the Association of Certified Fraud Examiners, 75% of companies that were victims of an internal fraud use external audits as an anti-fraud measure. Fifty-nine percent of victim companies use internal audits to help prevent fraud, and 46% utilize fraud training to combat fraud.[a]

[a]2006 Report to the Nation, Association of Certified Fraud Examiners, Austin, TX.

An *anonymous reporting mechanism*, such as an employee fraud hotline, is one way to maintain control. If employees take the hotline seriously, believe they will truly remain anonymous, are encouraged to use it, and see action taken based on anonymous reports, they will be more likely to make use of it. It is important that unreliable tips be weeded out quickly, so that efforts can be focused on the legitimate information provided. For the reporting mechanism to be taken seriously, employees need to see that appropriate action is in fact being taken, to the extent that it is legal and practical.

IN THE REAL WORLD

Effectiveness of Anonymous Hotlines

According to the Association of Certified Fraud Examiners, organizations that had fraud hotlines or other anonymous reporting mechanisms suffered median internal fraud losses only half as large as those that did not have them. Companies with hotlines had median losses of $100,000, whereas those without had median losses of $200,000.[a]

[a]2006 Report to the Nation, Association of Certified Fraud Examiners, Austin, TX.

The final common piece of the internal controls puzzle is the company's *monitoring activities*. Management can and should monitor access to computers, buildings, storage areas, and the accounting system. In this information age, it is necessary to monitor such things as email usage, attempts at cracking passwords, and changes or adjustments to accounts.

TIPS AND TECHNIQUES

Key Control Activities within a Company

- **Safeguards over assets.** Physical security and data security
- **Segregation of duties.** Not giving one person too much authority or access; having employees cross-check one another as a normal part of the process
- **Proper authorization.** Ensuring that transactions are properly authorized and that the rules related to authorization are enforced
- **Independent checks on performance.** Surprise audits and other internal analysis of compliance with policies and procedures
- **Anonymous reporting mechanism.** A hotline that is taken seriously and properly utilized by employees
- **Monitoring activities.** Examining and tracking access to computerized data, buildings, assets, and accounting systems

Fraud Prevention Framework

One proposed fraud prevention framework is a three-part program that is applied to every department and employee. This comprehensive fraud prevention program is not just a one-dimensional plan that focuses on accounting department activities; it must be implemented companywide for the best possible results.

Such a program can be expensive and can take months or years to implement fully. Furthermore, the most effective comprehensive fraud prevention program will not be a one-time project. It will require ongoing work as the company monitors the effectiveness of the program, makes updates to keep up with changes in operations and technology, and improves processes based on results of the program.

The three-part program includes fraud education, fraud investigations, and proactive fraud prevention techniques. All three ultimately depend on one another, so eliminating any one of them severely damages the framework and makes it wholly ineffective. Each section is divided into four major components, and the components are circular in that the completion of all four components starts the process over again.

TIPS AND TECHNIQUES

Comprehensive Fraud Prevention Program Components

- **Fraud education:** Teaching employees about fraud risks
- **Fraud investigation:** Investigating instances of suspected fraud
- **Fraud prevention:** Evaluating, designing, and implementing controls that proactively prevent fraud

Fraud Prevention: Education

The fraud education part of the program begins with an "introduction to fraud." All employees receive fraud awareness training, and in conjunction with this, management garners buy-in from the employees. Employees must believe that fraud prevention in general, and fraud education specifically, are important to them as individuals and to the company as a whole. Naturally, management and executives must be on board with the program as well. They set the tone for all other employees, so their cooperation is key to the implementation.

Fraud awareness training is important because studies have shown that employees are excellent corporate watchdogs, willing to report fraud if they know what to look for and have a way to notify management. It makes sense, then, to give them the tools they need to help in detecting fraud. Initially, all employees should be given one to two hours of training that introduces them to fraud, how it is committed, who perpetrates it, and what it looks like. On an ongoing basis, similar training should be given to new employees, and annual "update" training should be done for all employees.

Targeted training must then be done for departments and job functions that may have a higher incidence of fraud. Development of a training strategy is the first step, as it's necessary to determine who needs more than just the basics on fraud. The company should then develop the training program so that management knows what will be taught before the education process begins. Key employees may assist in creating the plan, along with the training programs and materials.

When the training strategy is being developed, it is important to determine the departments that are at greater risk for fraudulent activities and the departments that have a better chance of detecting fraud. Naturally, the finance and accounting functions will receive more training than other departments. Additional training may also be warranted for employees who deal with inventory control or other at-risk assets. Employees may receive several training sessions, depending on their job duties and the types of fraud they are likely to encounter.

One component of fraud education includes participative development of the education programs, as well as participation in the development of fraud prevention policies and procedures. So as employees are receiving training on fraud, they can also be encouraged to help develop preventive techniques. It certainly makes sense to solicit input from those on the front lines of the company. That knowledge can be used not only for the development of educational programs but to assist in the development of the fraud prevention procedures.

Quarterly workshops for updating fraud awareness training should be planned, rotating the employees so that they each participate in at least one workshop per year. Employees may be enlisted to train other employees. This can be a very effective teaching method when it is done by people who are motivated to help and who are experienced in public speaking.

Actually, designing the fraud prevention educational programs is not overly difficult if management brings in an anti-fraud professional who is experienced in these matters and if the focus remains on "the real world." That is to say, during educational sessions the focus is on the real situations that employees will encounter while on the job.

They don't need to learn a lot of theories about how and why fraud occurs. They need to know the reality about fraud, what it might look like at their company, how they might notice that something is wrong, what kind of tips are encouraged, and what will happen after they report a suspected fraud.

Anti-fraud education at a company should not be just another mandatory training class for employees. It should be a valuable session that can get the employees thinking about how they can help management detect and prevent fraud.

 TIPS AND TECHNIQUES

Designing an Anti-Fraud Education Program

- Introduction to fraud—a short primer on fraud and why it's so important for employees to learn about it
- Common ways that fraud could be committed at a company's place of business
- Discussion of areas of the company that are particularly vulnerable to fraud
- How fraud is detected—what to look out for and what constitutes suspicious behavior that should be reported
- How to report fraud; include anonymous reporting methods as well as in-person methods. Who should receive the information?
- What we do with tips about fraud—how tips are evaluated and the follow-up steps. How we protect the identity of the person who reported the suspected fraud
- Whom to contact if more information is need about fraud

Fraud Prevention: Investigation

The fraud investigation portion of the comprehensive fraud prevention program is necessary even if the company has truly effective fraud controls in place and rare occurrence of employee fraud. Ideally, the need for investigations will decrease as the preventive controls become more effective. Still, the need for investigations will never completely go away, given that some frauds will still occur and that investigations can provide a deterrent effect. When employees see that the company investigates suspicions of fraud, they are less likely to engage in it.

Fraud investigations were discussed in detail in Chapter 6, but some basics as they relate to the comprehensive program merit discussion. The first step in developing the investigation portion of the program is identifying the fraud indicators and the monitoring process. Management must be aware of the red flags that indicate fraud within the company, and develop a process for evaluating evidence and commencing an investigation.

Evaluating a fraud in the context of a company's internal controls is critical to the investigation part of the comprehensive fraud prevention program. Not many companies do this, but it can be instrumental in preventing future frauds. Conducting an investigation provides an ideal opportunity to examine the controls involved in the fraud. Which controls did or did not work in this situation? Why didn't they work, and how can they be improved? The investigators should evaluate additional controls that might have stopped the fraud and determine whether they would be practical to develop and implement.

After performing the investigation using the company's methodology, the results must be communicated to the appropriate parties.

In public companies, that will likely be senior management and the audit committee of the board of directors. In private companies, it will likely be the owner and the board of directors. Decisions about discipline and legal action must then be made, keeping in mind that disciplining those who steal from the company can have a deterrent effect on other would-be fraudsters.

The final critical piece of the investigation component of the comprehensive fraud prevention program is tracking the fraud incidents, analyzing what occurred and who was involved, analyzing the controls involved, and utilizing the findings to prevent future frauds. Each fraud yields competitive intelligence that can help management refine training, policies, and procedures and prevent future frauds.

Fraud Prevention: Proactive Prevention Techniques

The third portion of a comprehensive fraud prevention program consists of the *proactive fraud prevention techniques*. If the three portions were to be compared on the basis of cost, time, and effort involved, this would be the most significant part of the program. This is where all the internal controls are developed and put into place, and the cost and time commitment for this section may dwarf those of the investigation and education sections.

The process of developing appropriate internal controls within a company must always start with a risk assessment. If management does not know the risks, how could it possibly design controls to deal with them? Therefore, it's imperative not only to identify the risks faced by the company but to rank them according to their severity so that the most critical risks can be addressed first.

Every business faces many of the same general risks, particularly in the accounting systems. Common general risks include inventory control, proper recording of revenues, and over- or understatement of assets. There may also be risks that are common to companies in a particular industry. For example, telecommunications companies incur "line costs" and risk improper expensing of costs related to those lines, as seen in the WorldCom fraud.

Finally, there are company-specific risks. For example, if a company has a high debt level as compared with its competitors, the pressure to meet debt covenants and make debt payments may create certain financial statement risks. Company-specific risks can be operational, people-related, or related to the structure of the company.

Once the appropriate risks have been identified, management must develop a strategy to deal with them. This involves prioritizing the risks, determining which are the most risky, which could create the largest financial losses, which have regulatory importance, and which are the most urgent from an operational standpoint. Hopefully, the company already has some internal controls in place to deal with the risks identified, and the development of strategy will take into account the effectiveness of current controls.

Also important is identifying the risks that might require operational changes and determining the changes to which the employees might be most receptive. First making changes that will be received well by employees can help create early support for the fraud prevention program. Companies should determine some areas in which quick improvements can be made and positive results can be quickly seen. This can energize employees and help their buy-in to the idea of fraud prevention.

The following steps should be taken to ensure a thorough assessment of the risks and control activities within a company:

- **Step 1.** Ensure that those participating in the evaluation have a thorough understanding of the business.

- **Step 2.** Identify the functional areas to be assessed, and develop a process for ensuring that all areas are evaluated.

- **Step 3.** Identify significant accounts in the accounting system that will be evaluated, as well as the classes of transactions that must be examined.

- **Step 4.** Examine the company's financial reporting objectives and assess the risks surrounding them.

- **Step 5.** Acquire a detailed understanding of the company's current control activities, and test them to determine how they have been implemented, how they are working, and how they are affecting the numbers recorded in the accounting system.

- **Step 6.** Based on testing performed, determine the effectiveness of current control activities. Also, identify deficiencies and the financial statement assertions that may be affected by these deficiencies.

- **Step 7.** Evaluate the deficiencies and begin development of enhanced and new internal control activities.

This process should involve employees from throughout the company to the extent that it is practical and desirable to do so. Since all departments throughout the company will have new controls implemented, it is important that management seek buy-in and assistance from key employees. The key employees have first-hand knowledge of many of the risks and possible solutions, so they are a natural source of information in the development of fraud prevention procedures.

One way to look at the development of the strategy for creating and implementing the proactive prevention policies and procedures is as though it were a business plan. Actions to be taken include mapping out the goals and priorities and figuring out when these will be implemented, who will be involved and what their roles will be, and what outcomes are desired. This plan will be something that management updates on an ongoing basis, as the timing and participants are likely to change as the project progresses.

Developing and implementing preventive policies and procedures begins with the creation of a reporting mechanism. How will fraud be reported? This should include creating an anonymous hotline and distributing guidelines on reporting fraud to management. Managers and executives should make themselves available for reports of fraud and should appear receptive to these reports.

Then the hard work really begins. The development of the internal controls is the heart of the whole comprehensive fraud prevention program. These are developed in light of the identified risks and with applicable regulations in mind. The company should develop the policies and procedures using the methodical approach and timing developed in the strategic portion of the process.

Policies and procedures must be put into action, and it's advisable to develop a small set of procedures, implement those, and then develop another small set and implement those. This is better than spending hours and hours behind closed doors developing procedures and then trying to implement them all at once. By developing and then implementing a small set of procedures, management can receive feedback and see how things are going. Immediate adjustments can be made when creating the next set of procedures.

When implementing new internal control procedures, it's important that employees are instructed on the procedures, how they work, and what their role is. Management should also consult with employees during the implementation process to determine whether any of the procedures are unworkable or inefficient. It is appropriate to revise the procedures as they're being implemented if something that looked good on the drawing board doesn't seem to work well in reality.

Formal evaluation of the policies and procedures is the final part of putting proactive fraud prevention into motion. It is critical to determine whether or not employees are following the new rules, and to be able to monitor compliance on an ongoing basis.

If employees are not following the new procedures, management must determine why. Is it because the procedures are impractical or impossible in practice? Are they too complex? Is an employee just noncompliant? Is the control deemed to be ineffective? Management needs to evaluate the answers to these questions and throw out the procedures in question if they're not working, improve them if necessary, or take action against the noncompliant employee. If the controls are deemed effective, is there an opportunity to make them even better and more effective?

When all this has been completed, it is time to go back to the start and reassess the internal controls. First on the list are new areas of the business. If the business and operations have changed since the company started the process of implementing the comprehensive fraud prevention program, those areas need to be evaluated first.

Reassessing existing business and operations should not be nearly as time consuming or expensive as it was the first time around. Management should be maintaining the program, not completely rewriting it. The company should consider creating an annual schedule for evaluating the effectiveness of controls in the various departments or functions. This type of planning spaces out the work and ensures that every department is kept current.

IN THE REAL WORLD

Designing and Implementing a Comprehensive Fraud Prevention Program

A large public company decided that the time was right to reevaluate the company's effectiveness at preventing fraud, and management wanted to go beyond Sarbanes Oxley in its efforts. It was determined that this would not be a "project." This was not going to be an activity to be feared, one that everyone hoped would be over soon.

Management took the approach that this was the new way business would be done. Fraud prevention would be an ongoing focus that wouldn't end once some new internal controls were established. Senior-level executives became involved immediately, telling employees face-to-face that the company was making changes for the better, and fraud prevention was a new focus that was here to stay.

Summary

Effective fraud prevention relies heavily on effective internal controls within a company. Internal controls are divided into preventive, detective, and corrective controls. Essentially, the controls will help a company stop fraud and detect it when it does occur.

Sarbanes-Oxley (SOX) has made it mandatory for public companies to evaluate and report on their internal controls over financial reporting. Specific control procedures are not dictated by SOX, for the most part. Additionally, the legislation doesn't necessitate many substantive improvements within companies.

In general, internal controls in companies should focus on safeguarding assets, segregating duties, ensuring proper authorization of transactions, independently checking on performance, allowing for the anonymous reporting of fraud, and monitoring the activities of employees.

An effective fraud prevention framework includes three core components: fraud education, fraud investigation, and proactive fraud prevention efforts. The educational component offers employees the opportunity to learn about fraud, how to identify it, and how to report it. The investigation component is focused on taking action when controls fail and employees commit and conceal fraud. The proactive prevention portion of the framework requires significantly more effort than the others and is aimed at assessing a company's risks and evaluating the control procedures. After that has been completed, management must design procedures and policies that specifically address and mitigate the fraud risks.

CHAPTER 8

Best Practices in Fraud Management

After reading this chapter, you will be able to

- Identify the most critical components of an effective corporate code of conduct.
- Develop an anonymous hotline for the reporting of suspected fraud.
- Apply best practices to the screening and management of employees.

When it comes down to it, executives are left to decide how to best prevent and control fraud within their companies. Those fraud prevention efforts must also include modifications to the way executives conduct business. We've seen that there are plenty of frauds committed by executive-level employees, and those are some of the most costly from a financial standpoint. Frauds by executives also have a high likelihood of damaging the reputation of a company, and that is a cost that must not be underestimated.

Given the realization that fraud will never be completely eliminated, and the reality that companies have limited budgets, managers must make strategic decisions regarding fraud prevention efforts. They take the actions that are most likely to have an immediate positive impact on fraud, while still being cost effective and easy to implement.

One of the single most effective means of reducing corporate fraud is anti-fraud education. Educating employees is attractive because it has been known to help reduce fraud and increase the detection of fraud, and at the same time it can be done relatively cheaply as compared with other preventive mechanisms. This is one way to jumpstart a company's fraud prevention efforts, and if it is done right, it can get a company's employees on board for what's about to come in the fraud-fighting future.

Fraud Awareness Training

In creating and developing an honest corporate culture, fraud awareness training for all employees is critical. The statistics show that training employees about fraud helps to decrease the occurrence of fraud in companies as well as to increase the likelihood of detecting fraud. Employees must be aware of what is and is not acceptable in their behavior. If they aren't educated, they have no way of knowing what is permitted.

Fraud awareness training should include information on how fraud affects both the company and the employees. General fraud schemes should be presented, and employees should be educated on the types of frauds they might see while doing their jobs. Employees should be made aware of the options available to them for reporting fraud, whether it is through an anonymous hotline or direct reporting to a member of management. It should be stressed that the company has a "zero tolerance policy" toward fraud, and the consequences for unethical behavior should be clearly mapped out and explained.

Creating and Instilling a Culture of Integrity

Among the options for creating an overall system or program for reducing fraud across the board in a company, the development of a corporate culture that does not tolerate fraud is probably the most effective. Of course, it is not just the development of a culture that is important; instilling it in the employees is crucial. Employees must be as committed to the ethical culture as management and must be willing to live it each day at work.

It's important to remember that creating a culture is not something that is done only for a short period of time. It is not a "project" that ends after a few months. The true "development" of a culture often takes years and is something that requires constant attention to maintain.

But it's worth it. At the end of the day, all the regulations in the world and all the rules that can be piled on the employees won't really stop them from committing fraud. Sure, there are procedures that can be implemented to reduce and prevent fraud. But a sufficiently motivated and creative employee can always find a way to commit fraud.

Fraud is truly prevented when employees and managers understand and believe that ethics are a core component of a company's business methods. It takes a combination of generally honest people, reasonable rules, and a commitment to a fraud-free environment to really prevent fraud in the long term.

The active involvement of senior management in the development of this ethical corporate culture cannot be underestimated. Employees regularly look to senior managers to model appropriate behavior at work. Executives and managers must be committed to creating an ethical culture and performing ethically each day at work.

Code of Ethics

A code of ethics is not a one-size-fits-all proposition. The idea of buying a ready-made ethics policy to apply to a company is a bad idea. Although it may help to have some materials that guide management through the process of developing an ethics policy and a code of ethics, each company has a unique culture and, therefore, unique needs.

The best ethics policies are not necessarily filled with rule after rule describing specific situations. Rather, good ethics policies address general conduct and promote an ethical corporate culture, providing a small number of examples as needed to demonstrate the application of the rules. It's impossible to create a rule for every situation that may arise, so codes of ethics should not be aimed at specifically defining each and every ethical dilemma that may occur.

A good code of conduct should address the following general issues and topics:

- **General employee conduct while at work.** Make it clear that the company generally expects ethical and honest behavior at work, and expects that employees will give their best efforts on behalf of the company.

- **Conflicts of interest.** Give clear examples of conflicts of interest in case employees aren't aware of what constitutes a conflict. For example, some employees may not be aware that doing business with one's brother's company could create a conflict, and certain guidelines should be followed. Distinguish between acceptable conflicts of interest (those that are disclosed and monitored) as opposed to those that are unacceptable.

- **Confidentiality.** Address confidentiality issues within the company (sharing information with other employees or departments) as well as issues connected with sharing information with people outside the company.

- **Relationships with customers and suppliers.** What goes beyond an acceptable professional relationship? If an employee is "friends" with a customer or supplier, how will that be handled? Must it be disclosed? Is it the company's policy to assign a different employee to the account?

- **Gifts.** What may be received, if anything, from outsiders or from people within the company? Both the dollar value that is acceptable and the type of gift that that may be allowed should be addressed.

- **Entertainment.** What types of entertainment activities are allowed with customers and vendors, and how often may these events occur? A sporting event may be an acceptable event with a customer, but a trip to a gentlemen's club may be considered inappropriate. Make these distinctions clear.

- **Unethical behavior.** It's important to define ethics and to outline certain behaviors that are unacceptable and strictly prohibited. Strictly prohibited behaviors may include taking kickbacks or bribes, giving confidential information to parties outside the company, or falsifying employment documents.

- **Using the organization's assets for personal activities.** Address the company's stance on using company resources (Internet access, office supplies, copiers, and vehicles) for personal purposes. Many companies allow some limited use of company computers and copiers for personal purposes, but the boundaries need to be clearly defined. The same should go for more valuable assets owned by the company, such as vehicles or credit cards.

- **Reporting fraud or unethical behavior.** Encourage employees to report their suspicions; the company can follow up on them and determine whether further investigation is needed. Employees should be aware that nothing is considered "too small" to be reported, and if it is a minor matter, management can just resolve it quickly and quietly. Stress an open-door policy and the availability of the fraud hotline, the supervisors, and the managers going up the chain of command.

Anti-fraud training must include education on the ethics policy. The code of conduct must be explained and demonstrated, and employees should be given a chance to ask questions both publicly and in private. It is dangerous to assume that an employee can read the code of conduct and automatically understand all of its provisions. Examining the code of conduct during fraud awareness training is time well spent.

Employees should affirm their receipt and understanding of the policy with an annual acknowledgment. It is a good idea to repeat the ethics policy training each year when these acknowledgments are due, in order to point out any changes or enhancements to the policy and to make employees aware of the new provisions.

A good code of ethics is not worth anything if the company does not enforce its provisions. It is necessary to implement consequences for violations of the code, and those consequences must reach all levels of employees. Disciplinary options should be clearly communicated to employees, and a consistent and fair application of the rules and consequences is key.

TIPS AND TECHNIQUES

Ethics Policy Checklist

- **Background.** Explain the intent behind creating the code of ethics.
- **Scope.** What and who does the ethics policy apply to? The policy should apply to suspected irregularities involving employees, as well as to outside parties such as vendors, consultants, shareholders, and the like.
- **Policy.** Describe what fraud is and that management will be responsible for the detection and prevention of fraud. Instruct

employees on how to report instances of suspected fraud or suspicious behavior.

- **Actions deemed to be fraud.** Describe general behaviors that are prohibited because they are considered fraudulent, such as the misappropriation of assets, divulging confidential information to third parties, or seeking compensation from vendors for offering them a contract. This section must strike a balance between thoroughly defining general instances of fraudulent behavior, and going overboard with hundreds of points.

- **Whom to contact.** Offer employees a contact person if they need clarification about whether or not a certain act is considered fraud.

- **Confidentiality.** Explain the company's policy with regard to tips and investigation results. It is suggested that the company share information from tips with only those who need to know.

- **Reporting procedures.** Explain the process for reporting instances of suspected fraud. Detail who should receive complaints and how anonymous tips may be reported. Discuss what happens after the tip has been received.

- **Disciplinary action.** Briefly explain what action might be taken if an investigation reveals evidence of fraud. Keep this section very general with some ranges of discipline.

Tone at the Top

The actions of those at the top of a company influence the actions of those below. In many cases, the actions of an executive become the model for behavior of the subordinates.

This is why when trying to create an ethical culture within a company, it is so important that senior managers exhibit integrity and transparency in everything they do.

Executives can be instrumental in the successful deployment of new anti-fraud initiatives and policy changes. Their "front-and-center" support and promotion of new initiatives can mean the difference between success and failure.

It has been shown time and again that when the senior-level executives demonstrate their adherence to the code of ethics, employees in general are more likely to follow the rules too. Executives should be actively involved in the development and deployment of anti-fraud initiatives in order to send a strong message to employees.

IN THE REAL WORLD

Tone at the Top

A worldwide beverage producer was implementing a new ethics policy and compliance programs. Senior management was very involved in this implementation, primarily with leading by example and holding employees accountable for compliance. The new ethics program was kicked off with a speech from the company's chief executive officer (CEO). He made it clear that he believed in this new ethics program and would see to it that all employees complied.

His words were not empty promises, and employees found out quickly that he meant business. Employees who didn't return their ethics compliance forms promptly were contacted by the CEO personally to find out why they hadn't completed them. At many company meetings and gatherings, the CEO mentioned the new ethics program, his support of it, and his commitment to making sure all employees complied.

Anonymous Hotlines

The Sarbanes-Oxley Act of 2002 (SOX) requires public companies to have an "anonymous reporting mechanism" in place for employees to report fraud. Most often, companies have an anonymous hotline to address this requirement. Studies have shown that anonymous hotlines are an effective fraud prevention and fraud detection tool, so the inclusion of this element in SOX was wise.

It is probably easiest and most effective for companies to contract with a company specializing in fraud hotlines. There are companies that provide excellent hotline services at reasonable prices. Outside companies also offer the employees added confidence that the hotline is truly anonymous.

If a company decides to implement its own in-house hotline, many issues will arise. The company must have a dedicated phone number and possibly additional contact options such as an email account or a website. Each reporting method must be continuously monitored so that information submitted is examined quickly.

Employees must be reassured that internal methods of reporting fraud are truly anonymous and confidential. This means that employees need to know how caller ID, email tracking, and Internet technologies are dealt with by the company. If an employee fears her or his identity will be revealed during the reporting process, the number of reports is likely to go down.

The in-house hotline must have trained employees responding to communications and evaluating information reported. A voicemail system for receiving tips may be sufficient, but a live person receiving a phone call can do much more to gather information, ask questions, and reassure an uneasy employee.

The company should have a formalized case management system to track the action taken after receiving a fraud tip. An employee who offers a tip on suspicious behavior should have a way to follow up on the report and receive status updates. The case management system should include clear guidelines on initiating investigations based on tips. Those receiving the fraud reports must know whom to contact to forward communications from employees.

Companies should consider disseminating information about the hotline to outside parties that might be in a position to report suspicious behavior. For example, an outside vendor may have information that a company's purchase agent is soliciting kickbacks in exchange for awarding contracts to the vendor.

Finally, management should regularly evaluate the effectiveness of the hotline and make improvements accordingly. If the hotline is not being used much, management should determine whether employees are distrustful of the process and should then solicit suggestions for improving the hotline. Management should also consider whether employees have been properly educated about the establishment and use of the hotline.

TIPS AND TECHNIQUES

Things to Consider When Creating an Internal Fraud Hotline

- Do you have a dedicated phone number, email system, or website for collecting information?
- Is your reporting system continuously monitored so that reports of fraud are addressed quickly?
- Do employees believe that the reporting system is truly anonymous?
- Are trained employees evaluating and responding to fraud tips?
- Might employees respond better to a live person rather than a voicemail system?
- Have employees been educated as to the function and proper use of the hotline?
- Has a case management system been developed to ensure that employee tips are being forwarded to the proper parties for follow-up?
- Are employees able to receive status updates about their fraud complaints?
- Is the fraud hotline available to outside parties?
- Is management regularly evaluating the effectiveness of the fraud hotline?

Creating a Positive Work Environment

A positive working environment can promote ethical behavior among employees. When employees feel secure in their jobs and valued as people, they are less likely to justify stealing from the company. If they further believe that it is okay to voice concerns about their jobs and the workplace, it will also help them feel valued and respected. In turn, this belief that they are valued as people and employees will help decrease motivators for fraud.

An open-door policy with employees tells them that you care about them and you value their input. Giving employees an option to talk to someone if they are having problems or feel pressured is a positive step. This can help in the case of employees who might be motivated to commit fraud because of pressure, either in their personal life or their work life. Allowing them a voice about issues at work, such as feelings of inequality or feeling overworked, will make it less likely that an employee will use feelings of unfairness as a justification for committing fraud.

Employees value flexible rules, responsive management, job security, and job stability. They do not appreciate continual crisis situations or negative and oppressive work environments. Managers should keep these things in mind when they try to create a positive and supportive work environment. They should try to put themselves in the shoes of the employee and ask themselves how the company's policies and procedures might be interpreted.

Another positive step is to implement simple anti-fraud techniques such as job rotations and mandatory vacations. Employees are less likely to find themselves involved in a long-term fraud when these basic techniques are applied.

Employee assistance programs can help minimize the likelihood of internal fraud. A perceived pressure is one-third of the fraud triangle. Offering tools to help employees cope with life and work pressures may keep them (hopefully) from turning to fraud to address their issues.

Managing the Fraud Risk

As with any area of the company, when it comes to fraud, management must measure the cost of potential losses against the risk of fraud occurring. Even with excellent fraud prevention controls in place, no company can be completely free from fraud. Therefore, insurance coverage for employee theft losses is an important part of anti-fraud best practices.

Basic coverage against fraud losses in many business policies will cover against fraud committed by the company's employees, usually with a deductible and a smaller policy limit. The basic coverage often does not cover acts by people outside the company, so separate coverage must be obtained to cover acts of vendors, directors, or other outside parties.

In addition, it's advisable to increase coverage beyond standard policy limits. As any company that has experienced an internal fraud will state, the policy limits will be quickly exhausted if a scheme continues for any length of time. It pays to investigate the cost of additional coverage.

Another optional coverage includes indirect and consequential losses caused by employee dishonesty. Under this category are such things as lost profits, lost business opportunities, investigative costs, and legal fees. These items are not covered by the standard policies, but companies can usually purchase this coverage separately. It's no secret that the costs to investigate and prosecute an internal fraud can escalate quickly, so this might be a worthwhile option.

Hiring the Right Employees

If true fraud prevention comes down to developing and enforcing an ethical corporate culture, hiring the right employees is critical. Even though studies show that most people who commit internal fraud don't have prior histories of committing fraud, it is still important to look into the backgrounds of potential employees.

To the extent allowable by law, it is important to do criminal records checks, especially on people who are applying for sensitive positions. Drug screening has become fairly standard, and is not a bad idea, considering the link between addictions and the propensity to commit fraud.

Verifications of credentials, past employment, and references are critical parts of the employment process that are (surprisingly) not always done. Any dishonesty that occurs in the hiring process should be regarded as a huge red flag, and the only way to discover that dishonesty is by verifying the information presented by the candidate. In today's business world, verification of education and certificates is mandatory, because technology has made it very easy to create counterfeit documents.

TIPS AND TECHNIQUES

Employment Checklist

- Criminal records
- Drug screening
- Credential verification
- Employment verification
- Reference checks

IN THE REAL WORLD

Verification of Credentials

An engineering firm fired a manager-level employee for misconduct on the job, and he subsequently was accused of stealing trade secrets and sensitive company information. A background check on the former employee revealed that he did not have the engineering degree he cited on his résumé prior to becoming employed with the company. Had management verified his credentials before hiring him, he probably would not have been hired, because of the false information on the résumé. If he hadn't been hired, he also wouldn't have had the opportunity to steal trade secrets and sensitive information.

Coming Full Circle

Fraud management is not a simple process. There is no one method, technique, or control that prevents fraud. It is a combination of education, discipline, modeling ethical behavior, and development of preventive controls that can reduce fraud. To suggest that there is anything straightforward or easy about that process would be silly.

Experts estimate that up to 75% of corporate frauds may go undetected. We'll never know the exact figure, as the fact that the frauds are undetected means that we don't know about them. Therefore, managing fraud also includes attempting to prevent those previously undetected frauds.

There are many actions that should be taken by management, and only a limited amount of time and resources are available to do so. As management balances the risks of fraud and the costs of prevention efforts, the most important thing is to start making progress. If companies begin to move in the right direction and begin to see progress, that is an ideal way to move toward effective fraud management. The fraud prevention programs can be developed over time.

Summary

Time and again, we see that educating employees about fraud is one of the most basic and most effective anti-fraud measures. Training programs must include information on the company's ethics policy to ensure that employees have a good understanding of the rules management expects them to follow. The ethics policy is part of a larger corporate culture that values and demands ethical behavior. Companies are served well by efforts to develop this ethical culture over time, and by management's strict adherence to ethical standards in a very public manner. Executives must lead by example, and this leadership in regard to ethics is critical.

The development of an anonymous hotline is important, especially if a company is subject to SOX. It may be easiest and most cost-effective to outsource the hotline to a third-party provider. A company that decides to develop a fraud hotline from within must ensure that it is secure and reliable. The identity of those reporting fraud must be protected, and the systems must be in place to log and manage complaints, as well as to appropriately follow up on them.

Hiring the right employees and creating a positive work environment are two keys to reducing corporate fraud. With the right employees in place, an ethical culture is more likely to be achieved. In a positive work environment that values people and their efforts, employees will be less motivated to commit fraud.

CHAPTER 9

The Future of Fraud

After reading this chapter, you will be able to

- Identify some of the most basic causes of corporate fraud.
- Understand the effect Sarbanes–Oxley and other modern legislation has had on fraud in businesses.
- Be aware of some of the most promising ways for companies to prevent fraud in the long-term.

Since the start of the current century, the focus on fraud has continued to increase. The public at large has become generally more aware of the issue of fraud, although maybe not overly knowledgeable about its methods and frequency.

Fraud is being studied more heavily by academics and by professional services firms. This focus on fraud can hardly be a bad thing.

The more attention the topic gets, the more likely that fraud prevention methods and tools will become more sophisticated and more effective. As time goes on, anti-fraud professionals are also developing their fraud-fighting skills and are able to better assist companies in detecting and preventing fraud.

But as we learned early on in this book, companies are currently out of touch with the effectiveness of their fraud prevention efforts. Management believes that newer internal controls, policies, and procedures have been effective in reducing fraud, but still there has been no substantive decrease in the occurrence or cost of fraud worldwide.

Until companies face the reality of their fraud situations, things won't improve. It is only by acknowledging and examining the deficiencies in systems that companies will be able to decrease their exposure to occupational fraud.

Root Causes of Fraud

We have already examined the many pieces of the fraud puzzle that go into the decision to commit fraud and the subsequent act of committing the fraud. The are many variables, but when it comes to the big frauds that make the headlines, one of the most common themes is the short-term pressure on executives to meet earnings targets. Constant market pressure to increase share prices is an overriding factor in most companies, and fraud prevention efforts may take a backseat in importance.

Investors are looking for a return on their capital investments in the short term, and this could push management to create aggressive and possibly unethical accounting practices to increase current earnings. In some ways, the marketplace condones fraud so long as earnings and stock prices increase. Unless investors object to putting earnings and share price ahead of fraud prevention, companies will not change their operational practices.

Enron may forever be a case study illustrating a company's dedication to the stock price. It's clear that the financial statement fraud at Enron started relatively small, and was done to conceal a quarter that wasn't going to meet analysts' expectations. Quarter after quarter, the financial statement fraud grew in magnitude because Wall Street expected continuous revenue growth from the company. When revenue wasn't there, Enron executives created fictitious revenue, and the share price responded with each successive quarter.

Compounding this short-term growth problem is the fact that senior management compensation is often tied closely to stock price. Granting stock options and awarding bonuses increases the pressure for positive financial results. If financial targets can be met in the absence of extensive fraud prevention controls and policies, executives have essentially met the objectives laid out for them.

One further complication is the fact that greed is a part of human nature. Greed on the part of executives may lead to the manipulation of earnings. Stories abound of executives using public companies as their own personal piggy banks. From senior managers buying lavish home furnishings on their employers' dime to executives making huge sums from stocks traded with insider information, the temptation and opportunity to commit fraud may be overwhelming.

Regulating Fraud

As larger frauds came to light, seemingly one after another, faith in the executives and financial statements of companies was rocked to the core. Regulations were implemented to help restore that faith and direct the business practices of companies. While the publicity and the regulations have altered the way companies do business, how significant is that effect and how long will the effect last?

Some think that tighter regulations for public companies and auditing firms will do a lot to prevent and reduce fraud. Yet recent history has shown that regulation is not necessarily the answer to the fraud problem.

The Sarbanes-Oxley Act of 2002 (SOX) was implemented quickly as a reaction to the major frauds at Enron, Tyco, and World-Com. Although the intent behind the legislation was good, it has been extremely costly to implement, and some doubt that the benefits have justified the high price tag.

The legislation was intended to help protect retail investors in public companies by bringing certain standards to the financial reporting process. SOX requires the executives and directors of the company to certify financial results, which holds them responsible for the accuracy and completeness of the financial data.

SOX also put into place provisions that were intended to give investors more confidence in the audit reports issued by audit firms. It created tighter rules related to auditor independence and the services provided to audit clients. The legislation was intended as a step toward preventing fraud in public companies, but opinions on the results vary widely.

Rules Under Sarbanes-Oxley

SOX created the Public Company Accounting Oversight Board (PCAOB), which is a private, not-for-profit entity that reports to the Securities and Exchange Commission (SEC). This organization is focused on providing useful and independent audit reports to the public. To this end, the PCAOB registers public accounting firms, sets quality and ethical standards for the issuers of audit reports, inspects registered public accounting firms, and leads investigations into and disciplinary actions against auditors.

Under SOX, companies must assess their internal controls, which are the policies and procedures that ensure the accuracy of financial data. In practice, public companies have spent thousands of hours documenting procedures and their effectiveness. The legislation does not explicitly require companies to improve their internal controls, but if a company has significant deficiencies in this area that remain uncorrected, the public must be notified.

SOX required changes to the boards of directors of public companies. It made it mandatory for companies to have outside, independent directors. It also required companies to have a "financial expert" on the audit committee of the board of directors. The legislation also included increased prison terms for those involved in financial statement fraud, accelerated reporting requirements for insider trading, and requirements to establish a whistleblower program to allow employees to report wrongdoing and fraud anonymously.

SOX prohibits auditors of public companies from engaging in other consulting work for those companies. In the past, the audit was often used as a "loss leader" to reel in a new client, with the hope of picking up more lucrative consulting work from the client later. Although audits are supposed to be an "independent" examination of the financial statements of a company, audit firms had their true independence questioned because of the amount of work done on behalf of companies and the huge fees generated from that work. With significant revenue on the line, is an audit firm really willing to hold a company's feet to the fire on a financial reporting issue and risk losing the company's business altogether?

Sarbanes-Oxley in Practice

Companies are required under SOX to evaluate their internal controls. The objective of internal controls is to give users of the financial statements reasonable assurance that the financial statements are reliable and corporate assets are secure.

If a company does not have effective controls in place, it may be required to report a material weakness, which signifies that there is more than a remote likelihood that a material misstatement in the financial statements will not be prevented or detected. Notice that a company is not necessarily required to correct the problem, as long as management is willing to report the weakness to the public.

It is clear that SOX has created some positive benefits for public companies and their investors. When companies were compelled to evaluate their internal control processes and procedures, deficiencies were brought to light and proactive companies corrected them. Not all companies corrected the problems, however. Users of financial statements should not be fooled into thinking that SOX has solved all of the financial reporting problems.

Companies have also cited new operational efficiencies and cost savings that can be tied to SOX work. In addition to improving the reliability of the financial reporting process, some companies took advantage of the opportunity to improve operations as well.

However, the legislation itself is *not* a fraud prevention tool. It mandated that certain improvements be made and certain actions be taken. Still, SOX did not require the implementation of internal controls that would create a long-term reduction in fraud.

Since the independent auditors of a public company are now prohibited from providing consulting services to that company, audit firms have changed how they conduct business. In theory, the auditors are now more independent in their work. Therefore, while the audit firms still rely on the payment of fees by clients, the sole focus on providing an audit may have increased the level of skepticism and independence maintained by the auditors.

Corporate governance has been improved as a result of SOX. Boards of directors have become more involved, and more informed on financial matters. Audit committees have become more proactive in policing the activities of companies and executives. All in all, there is more oversight of the executives and more analysis of the financial results of companies, which are undeniably positive results of the legislation.

The current legislation has also increased prison sentences for executives engaged in fraudulent activities. However, these longer sentences are not likely to have a significant deterrent effect. An executive who commits fraud generally does so with the expectation that she or he will not be caught. Therefore, the executive is unlikely to compare old and new prison sentences when considering whether or not to commit fraud.

Critics of Sarbanes-Oxley

Some critics of SOX say that the legislation was done in haste in an attempt to quickly allay the fears of the investing public. They maintain that some provisions of the legislation do not work as well as they should and need changing. Critics have called SOX "overregulation" and shortsighted, and since its inception, there have been many proposals regarding changes and improvements to it.

It has been suggested that the small improvements at companies came at too high a price. Most will admit that there were improvements at companies that implemented SOX, but that the improvements were really just incremental and not sufficiently effective to justify the price tag.

A 2006 survey by Financial Executives International (FEI) on SOX showed that compliance costs have decreased but remain substantial. FEI surveyed 200 companies, that had average revenues of $6.8 billion. The average cost for annual SOX compliance in 2006 was $2.9 million, a decrease of 23% from the prior year's survey. It appears, then, that companies are becoming more efficient in complying with SOX; still, the costs are significant.

The survey by FEI also confirmed one of the primary criticisms of SOX: the cost-versus-benefit issue. Just under 50% of survey respondents believed that their financial reports were more accurate and more reliable. Increased accuracy and reliability is good, but 78% of survey respondents told FEI that the cost of compliance exceeds the benefits.

Unintended Consequences

SOX critics further maintain that the legislation has created a situation that is even worse than it was without any legislation. They fear that this law has been mostly misinterpreted by the general public and therefore may do more harm than good.

If investors and users of financial statements mistakenly believe that Sarbanes-Oxley has caused companies to make great strides in preventing fraud, they may be caught off guard. A false sense of security when it comes to the existence of fraud cannot be a good thing. In fact, it may mean that the public is actually worse off than it was before the legislation came into effect.

Regulating Accounting Firms

Public accounting firms that perform independent audits are also subject to a lengthy list of rules and regulations governing their work. These auditing standards require the auditors to be truly independent with respect to the companies being audited; they also specify some quality control procedures.

Overall, these standards for auditors are a good idea. However, they do not really do a lot to enhance the detection and prevention of fraud. Audits are not designed to find fraud, and therefore regulations of auditors to date haven't done much about fraud either.

Alternatives to Legislation

Could similar positive results have been achieved with something other than the Sarbanes-Oxley legislation? Was legislation even the answer at all?

At the very least, critics are suggesting that changes should be made to SOX, particularly as they relate to the cost of compliance. They say that the regulation went too far in terms of requirements and related costs, and that it unfairly penalizes business as a whole for the well-publicized bad acts of certain executives at certain companies.

It is reasonable to propose changes that make compliance easier and less costly. The costs of complying with Sarbanes-Oxley have been burdensome, and it only makes sense that the legislation should be revisited and improved to find a better balance between costs and benefits. Those proposing changes should be careful what they wish for, however, as there is no guarantee that a modified SOX won't be worse than what is already in place.

Closing Thoughts

When one looks critically at the regulatory efforts aimed at curbing fraud, it is easy to come to the conclusion that regulation is really not the answer. Dishonest people will commit fraud and other crimes if they can get away with it, laws or no laws.

Even with extensive fraud examinations and effective internal controls, dishonest executives may always find a way to commit fraud. They can override controls or engage in even more creative practices to cover up theft. Only a shift in ethics and values could stop this. The greedy executive who wants to meet earnings targets cannot be stopped by even the best controls and examinations.

Companies would be better served by addressing the fraud issues specific to their own companies, and then developing an "ethical corporate culture" that will serve them well in the long run. Proactive fraud prevention efforts are most certainly more worthwhile than a check-the-box process that is aimed primarily at meeting the requirements of regulations.

By developing a customized, comprehensive fraud prevention effort with the assistance of trained and experienced anti-fraud professionals, management can decrease a company's likelihood of being victimized by fraud. At the very least, the company may well decrease the opportunities for fraud and increase the chances of its early detection.

But if regulations aren't holding companies and executives accountable, who will? The stakeholders of companies will force them to solve the problem of fraud if it becomes costly enough. Shareholders, employees, lenders, and other interested parties will be called on to hold companies to higher standards than in the past. Ethical behavior will be rewarded by the marketplace if the marketplace deems it important.

Companies that do business in a reckless manner and executives who are not held accountable will be punished by the marketplace if it is deemed sufficiently important. The parties impacted negatively by fraud will demand changes and will speak with their support and their money. Constant pressure on companies to mitigate the risk of fraud is necessary to force them to remain focused on good fraud prevention controls and protection of investors.

Index